Without Regret

A Handbook for Owners of Canine Amputees

Susan Neal

Published by Doral Publishing, Sun City, Arizona
Printed in the United States of America.

Edited by SageBrush Publications
Interior Design by The Printed Page
Cover Design by 1106 Design

Library of Congress Card Number: 2002103421
ISBN: 0-944875-85-8

Without Regret

A Handbook for Owners of Canine Amputees

For my sweet Izzy,
love you always

Acknowledgments

I would like to extend a deep and sincere thank you to Dr. Donna Chase of Town and Country Animal Hospital in New Boston, New Hampshire. Because of Dr. Chase, this book was made possible. Dr. Chase was the veterinarian who performed the flawless amputation for my sweet Izzy. Izzy never experienced a single complication due to her surgery, and Dr. Chase's work was so effective that all traces of the cancer that had afflicted Izzy were removed, and she was blessed with a very rare miracle—a cure. Dr. Chase not only saved Izzy's life but she gave her many, many wonderful, healthy years to share with her grateful family. Thank you, Donna, so much!

Dr. Chase also provided medical information regarding the criteria used by veterinarians in recommending amputation, as well as material on post surgical complications. She was exceedingly kind to review and critique a good deal of the manuscript prior to publication. Her assistance and input will always be greatly appreciated.

A special thank you to Carrie Haggart from Out To Pasture Farm and Rescue in Coventry, Connecticut. Carrie's rescue organization is a sanctuary for elderly, sick, and handicapped pets. She provided many wonderful photographs of canine amputees, which are used throughout this book. Thank you, Carrie, and keep up the wonderful work that you are doing!!

Of course, no acknowledgement would be complete without thanking the hundreds of amputee owners who sent me their stories, photos, and words of encouragement. Without you, this handbook would not have been so informative, personal, or well documented graphically. It was my desire to be able to include at least a brief mention, an anecdote, or a photo of every single amputee of whom I learned. However, there were some whose stories could not be told. During the five years that it took to bring this book to publication, I lost touch with a few folks and was not able to secure the necessary paperwork from them to use their stories. There were also a small number of contributors whose submissions, for reasons unrelated to their wonderful amputees, simply were not featured. I would like to take this opportunity to acknowledge them and their amputees. They are:

- *Bo* (English Springer spaniel) owned by Peg Fletcher
- *Brady* (English setter) owned by Deborah Ramsey
- *Ila* (Mixed breed) owned by Shannon Horton
- *Foxie* (Husky) owned by Cindy Duchemin
- *Fawn* (German shepherd mix) owned by Mr. and Mrs. John Burney
- *Kamoosh* (Golden retreiver) owned by Henrietta Focht
- *Cassie* (Boxer mix) owned by Cynthia Davis
- *Ace* (Labrador retreiver) owned by Marc Reddy
- *Peggy* (Pitbull mix) owned by Bob & Jana Ventura
- *Dexter* (Lab/Husky mix) owned by David Rosenthal
- *Hope* (Mixed breed) owned by Susan Bartis
- *Hopalong Cassidy* (Labrador retreiver) owned by Bonnie Brayshaw
- *Elsa* (Lab mix) owned by Andrea Shaw Reed
- *Kasy* (Rottweiler) owned by Barbara Decker
- *Three* (Beagle) owned by Gary Eaton
- *Pumpkin* (Poodle) owned by Cheryl Yacono
- *Fred* (Mixed breed) owned by Bob Whatmough
- *Liberty* (Terrier mix) owned by Patsy Kohn
- *Skippy* (Beagle) owned by Karen Mazurek
- *Elsie* (Mixed breed) owned by Jean Miller
- *Tootsie* (Poodle) owned by Kimberly Krill
- *Pebbles* (English toy spaniel) owned by Jo La Fentres
- *Brody* (Border collie) owned by Eileen Brown
- *Missy* (Doberman) owned by Tracy Mingus
- *Spot* (Mixed breed) owned by Myrna and Irv Paris
- *Patrick* (German shepherd) owned by Heidi Gibb

Contents

Introduction

Why write a book on canine amputation? Many people have asked me this. Could there possibly be an audience? Why would anyone want or need a book on such a subject? These two questions are typically asked by someone who has either never owned a dog or who has never owned a disabled one. If you have picked up this book, then chances are you currently own an amputee or you are facing the prospect of becoming the owner of one. This book was written for you, and you know the answer to "why" it is needed. You love your dog and need answers about his or her life!

An impending limb amputation for your pet is uncharted territory for the average dog owner. You have probably never had to face such a momentous situation—that of allowing your beloved pet to be literally taken apart in order to save its life or improve the quality of its life. You may have discovered that regular veterinarians and other health care providers are of little help to you in this new chapter of your life. They have probably been very vague about what to expect from life with a canine amputee. This is not because they are reluctant to tell you, it is because they simply do not know themselves. Unless they have personally gone through this ordeal with a dog of their own, they simply do not understand all the challenges and questions that may arise. Yes, they are probably exceptional surgeons and can handle a limb amputation with ease, ensuring no complications during or after the surgery. They can stabilize the physical condition of the animal and provide treatments and courses of action to ensure that physical healing begins and continues in an orderly manner. But it is the emotional and spiritual healing of both the dog and the owner that truly needs the most attention. And *where* can you find the answers for the countless questions that are now running through your mind?

In addition to being unable to garner much helpful information from your animal's care providers, you have probably also found that your friends or family members do not understand what you are going through. Perhaps you have already encountered their unintentional insensitivity and misunderstanding in your search for the correct path to take in this decision. Your need to discuss your fears, hopes, and uncertainties may have fallen on uncaring ears. For some, the only answer to your inquiries has been something like, "It's only a dog. Just put it to sleep." These poor souls do not realize how deeply they may have wounded you, so do not hold it against them. Some may never have known the unconditional love of a devoted family pet. Others would never consider their dog a member of the family or a beloved "child," as many people do. Clearly, it is not from such individuals that you will find hope, encouragement, and enlightenment. You need to find a truly knowledgeable source. You need to know that there are others out there who feel as you do and that it is all right to feel this way. Most importantly, you need concise, useful answers to your questions. I hope that this book can be a place for you to start finding the answers you seek.

Who better to write a reference guide on owning a canine amputee than someone who has lived with one and been through what you are now facing? My journey along this unexpected path began in 1995 when my two-year-old bullmastiff female, Wiccaways Isabeau, was diagnosed with bone cancer. Based on recommendations from the local veterinary university, which proclaimed Izzy's bone cancer to be one of two very rare and slow-growing types, I agreed with my local vet that the only way to save her life was to amputate her right rear leg.

I soon found myself overwhelmed with questions, fears, and doubts about how this drastic physical change would affect my vivacious young dog. The lack of information and help was frightening. No one, not even my dedicated veterinarian, could give me any specific or helpful suggestions about how to live with a canine amputee…and a cancer victim to boot.

But Izzy herself was a patient and inspiring teacher. Though predicted to have a survival rate of only five months following her amputation, Izzy has valiantly beaten the odds and has lived a happy, healthy, pain-free life for the past five years. Her story is not unique. Every year in this country, more than thirty thousand dogs[1] become canine amputees. Every single one of them represents an amazing, touching, inspiring story. When I realized I might loose Izzy at any moment, I knew I had to do something to honor her life and ensure that she was never forgotten. I initially intended to produce a beautiful remembrance book about Izzy and her amazing tale. As I became involved in researching canine cancers and disabilities, and as the responses from hundreds of other amputee owners came pouring in with questions and pleas for information regarding this subject, I soon realized that what they truly needed was an informative, factual handbook to assist amputee owners, not just a pretty coffee-table book.

This work is intended as an introductory guide for the layperson in his or her search for knowledge regarding the health of his or her pet who is, or may soon become, a canine amputee. It is not intended as a comprehensive medical dissertation for practitioners, though the author hopes that they, too, can find useful information within these pages and increase their knowledge of this unique condition—if for no other reason than to be able to offer their clients

---

1   Based on the author's estimates.

compassion and understanding during what may be the most trying time in many pet owners' lives.

While this book has been written to hopefully inform, educate, and comfort other dog owners and professionals within the animal health care industry, it is because of Izzy that I have written it. It simply would not exist without her. Her unfailing spirit and her miraculous existence encourage me at all times. Her life—and my choices for her—have been completely *Without Regret*.

Chapter 1

The Canine Amputee and Its Owner

"Sprinter"   *Photo Chris Morway*

Barney enjoying a romp in the yard.   *Photo Diane Paquin*

So who is the typical canine amputee? Can assumptions be made as to which dogs may or may not be ultimately affected by this disability? In some cases, the answer, surprisingly, is yes. For example, dogs that are allowed to run loose are certainly prime candidates for this type of disability—or worse. In general, unlike other canine disabilities such as blindness or deafness, it is very difficult to say which dogs may become amputees. The one certain truth regarding this disability is that any dog, at any time, and for any number of reasons can suddenly become an amputee. This disability has no respect or predisposition for the pedigree of the dog, the social or economic class of its owner, the dog's age, sex, behavior, size, living environment, or state of health. Amputation can occur suddenly and unexpectedly or may be the final course of treatment after a prolonged illness or injury.

Among humans, the leading cause of amputation is from complications of diabetes. Other causes of human amputation include traumatic injury—typically auto accidents, cancer, and acts of war. Humans can be very severely affected by amputation because of our unique cultures. Human amputees are often plagued by thoughts and emotions pertaining to their loss of status within society (real or imagined). This can create extreme challenges in dealing with the reality of being an amputee. Common fears and questions that concern an amputee include: Will I lose my job or how will I now perform my job? How will I support my family? How will my friends and colleagues view me? Will I lose my social status, my degree of respect, my dignity? How will my spouse react to living with an amputee? Will my spouse leave me? Will I be able to once again engage in everyday activities? How will the disability limit my enjoyment of, or ability to engage in, sports, employment, exercise, hobbies, and daily life? The perceived obstacles facing a human amputee are many. This can create extreme behavioral problems such as depression, anger, self-pity, self-destructive tendencies—including thoughts of suicide, withdrawal from family and friends, and loss of interest in life.

Fortunately for dog owners, our pets are not plagued by such emotional baggage. Our dogs do not care how they will perform as a tri-ped; they simply go out and perform as best they can. They do not worry that their canine housemates may think less of them; their buddies seldom do. They certainly do not engage in debilitating bouts of self-pity and regret about what may have been and what can never be. They are amazing creatures who enjoy life in whatever manner they are allowed, who love their owners unconditionally, regardless of the decisions that have been made for them and the things that may have been done to them, and who harbor no fears about the uncertainties of the future.

Unlike human amputees, who sometimes do not fully recover from their amputation either emotionally or physically, the canine amputee recovers from his ordeal very swiftly and with little or no physical or emotional complications.

Of course, it is possible for a human owner to project his own fears and trepidations regarding this type of disability onto the dog. Animals are very sensitive to emotions, and they often pick up on their owners' feelings and may alter their behavior because of them. A dog that under normal circumstances might recover quickly and easily from amputation surgery may begin to exhibit abnormal or inappropriate behavior based solely on the negative emotions being projected by the owner. This typically happens in cases where the owner was not prepared for the reality of living with an amputee. Perhaps the person simply does not have the emotional fortitude to deal with the animal's initial physical needs. In some cases, the person is very preoccupied with physical appearances and is so consumed with human prejudices against anything "abnormal" or "handicapped" that he or she actually sends out signals of unworthiness and dislike to the pet. Even though the owner may be experiencing these emotions on a subconscious level and may not actually be acting out disappointment with the dog, the pet can recognize and interpret them nonetheless. The pet's response to such signals is often to behave as though he or she were being punished. Owners who are unhappy with their pet's physical appearance commonly note fear, avoidance, and depression in the animal. In the home of another owner, one without disability prejudices, the same pet, in all likelihood, would behave far differently. The dog is a keenly sensitive animal. The owner of a new amputee must be ever careful and vigilant not to allow his or her own fears and emotional baggage to hinder his or her pet's full recovery.

Human amputees benefit from the efforts of the National Limb Loss Information Center, Limb Loss Research and Statistics Program. This organization reports that there were 185,000 surgical amputations performed in 1996.[2] The National Amputation Foundation, founded in 1919 by veterans of World War I who had become amputees as a result of that war, offers human amputees valuable education, literature, and assistance. It provides a wealth of information to amputees and their families.

---

2   National Health Interview Survey, Series 13, No. 139

So how many dogs per year become amputees, and who are they? Unfortunately, there is no organization in the world that records such data for animals. Based on research conducted by the author, the number of dogs who become amputees every year may potentially be as high as thirty-seven thousand plus animals. There is no resource or organization to which dog owners can turn for help or information. The tables and notes that follow were compiled by the author from data provided by canine amputee owners during 1997-1998. Table 1 pertains to cancer cases, Table 2 to auto accidents, and Table 3 to injuries or diseases other than cancer or auto accident.

Table 1: Amputee Results—Cancer

Breed of dog	Age at time of injury	Sex of dog	Type of cancer
Doberman	12 years	male	osteosarcoma
Border Collie	2 years	male	unknown
Briard	1 year	male	osteosarcoma
Rottweiler	8 years	male	osteosarcoma
Labrador Retriever mix	6 years	female	unknown
Greyhound	6 years	male	unknown
Golden Retriever	4.5 years	male	osteosarcoma
Old English Sheepdog	9 years	male	osteosarcoma
German Shepherd	7 years	male	unknown
Greyhound	adult	female	osteosarcoma
Greyhound	5 years	male	osteosarcoma
Boxer	7 years	male	fibrosarcoma
Golden Retriever	6.5 years	male	unknown
Bedlington Terrier	7 years	female	mast cell tumor
Rottweiler	8 years	female	unknown
Lab/Rhod. Ridgeback	4 years	female	osteosarcoma
Belgian Shepherd	11 years	male	unknown
Golden Retriever	9 years	female	synovial sarcoma
Greyhound	8 years	female	osteosarcoma
Lab/Husky mix	8 years	male	unknown—rare
Husky/GSD mix	adult	male	unknown

Cancer Amputee Data
There are several conclusions that can be extrapolated from the above data.

1. Male dogs are twice as likely to be affected by cancer as are females.

2. Cancer is typically a disease affecting older or geriatric dogs. The average onset age is approximately seven years, well into advanced age for most dogs.

3. Cancer is a disease that affects mostly large or giant purebred dogs (50+ lbs.).

4. According to this data, osteosarcoma is by far the most prevalent form of bone cancer in dogs, accounting for approximately 81% of all cases; 19% of cases are classified as "rare" or "other."

5. One surprising fact is that so many respondents did not know the type of cancer that affected their dogs. This information is vitally important for dog owners because those cancers that are not osteosarcoma can have a fairly good prognosis if the owner follows the necessary treatment and care options prescribed for these diseases.

6. In comparing the above results to the total number of respondents, we find that there is statistical evidence to conclude that 25% of all canine amputations result from cancer related complications.

Table 2: Amputee Results—Auto Accidents

Breed of dog	Age at time of injury	Sex of dog	Type of auto injury
Labrador mix	2 years	female	unknown
Austr. Shepherd mix	2.5 years	male	unknown
German Shepherd mix	adult	male	unknown
Border Collie mix	adult	male	fall from vehicle
German Shepherd mix	1 year	female	unknown
Beagle	adult	male	hit by vehicle
Spitz mix	adult	female	hit by vehicle
Scottish Terrier	11 years	male	hit by vehicle
Lab/Dobie mix	1 year	female	unknown
Golden Retriever mix	1 year	female	hit by vehicle
Golden Retriever	< 1 year	male	hit by vehicle
Pitbull mix	8.5 years	female	hit by vehicle
Hound mix	adult	female	jumped from truck
Labrador Retriever	adult	male	hit by vehicle
Labrador mix	adult	female	crushing
Keeshound	4 years	male	hit by vehicle
Beagle	adult	female	dragged by vehicle
Labrador mix	adult	female	hit by vehicle
Terrier mix	4.5 years	female	hit by vehicle
Doberman	adult	female	hit by vehicle
Unknown mix	< 1 year	male	run over by vehicle
Malamute	< 1 year	female	hit by vehicle
Rottweiler	< 1 year	female	hit by vehicle
Labrador Retriever	1 year	male	run over by bus
Boxer	1 year	male	hit by vehicle/neglect
Border collie	adult	male	hit by vehicle
Labrador mix	2 years	male	hit by vehicle
German Shepherd	< 1 year	male	fall from truck
Boxer mix	adult	female	hit by vehicle

Auto Accident Amputee data

The above data supports the following findings regarding auto accident amputees:

1. Mixed breeds and mutts are at a slightly higher risk of being injured due to car accidents than are purebred dogs. This may be due to the fact that individuals who are willing to make a sizeable financial investment in a purebred may be more inclined to protect that investment and keep it safe than someone who received a dog for free or made only a minimal financial investment in that animal.

2. The average age for this type of injury (assuming that those dogs listed as "adult" are at least one year of age) is two years. These statistics are supported by the fact that a young dog can be rebellious, energetic, and at

times intractable. By providing proper training and supervision of a dog at this critical age, most such incidents can be easily avoided.

3. There is no predisposition for either sex to be injured in an auto-related accident. The girls are just as likely as the boys to act up at this young age and become seriously injured.

4. As can be readily seen, the most common way in which a dog is injured by a vehicle is when it is hit by one, as typically occurs when a dog is allowed to run loose or is left unsupervised. Nearly one hundred percent of canine amputations as a result of auto accidents are preventable, if the owners contain, control, or supervise their animals.

5. Auto accidents account for thirty-five percent of all canine amputations, based on the results of this survey.

Table 3: Amputee Results—
Other Than Cancer Or Auto Accidents

Breed of dog	Age at time of injury	Sex	Type of "other" injury
P.W. Corgi	2 days	female	whelp injury
English Setter	1 year	male	gunshot/fracture
Keeshound	adult	male	unknown
German Shepherd mix	adult	female	abuse
Husky mix	adult	female	unknown
German Shepherd mix	newborn/congenital	female	birth defect
German Shepherd mix	adult	male	unknown
Labrador Retriever	adult	female	unknown
Vizla	adult	male	unknown/birth defect
Eng. Springer Spaniel	4 months	male	parvo complication
Toy Poodle	2 years	female	abuse
Golden Retriever	4 years	male	breeder abuse/neglect
Australian Shepherd	newborn/congenital	female	birth defect
Husky/Terrier mix	adult	female	trap
German Shepherd mix	< 1 year	male	abuse/buckshot
Husky/GSD mix	5 years	female	barb wire
Pitbull	1.5 years	male	lawnmower
Norfolk Terrier	newborn/congenital	female	whelp injury
Amer. Staffordshire Terr.	1 year	female	fall from window
Maltese	7 years	female	gangrene
Saluki	newborn/congenital	female	birth defect
Lab/GSD mix	adult	female	trap
Santos	adult	female	abuse/neglect
Doberman	adult	female	abuse/dog fighting
Rottweiler	4 months	female	unhealed fracture
Husky mix	1 year	female	unhealed fracture
Toy English Spaniel	newborn/congenital	female	birth defect
Collie	2 days	female	whelp injury/dog bite
Pomeranian	adult	male	trap
Terrier mix	adult	female	unknown
Poodle mix	4 years	female	unknown
Pitbull	1 year	male	abuse
Toy Poodle	3 days	male	dog bite
Chihuahua	< 1 year	female	abuse

Amputee Data: Injuries or Diseases Other than Cancer or Auto Accidents
Due to the fact that there are so many different types of injuries or illnesses grouped together in this data field, definitive findings are somewhat harder to extrapolate.

1. The majority of very young dogs who become amputees are typically due to a congenital defect (almost exclusively among purebred dogs) or as the result of unsafe interaction between very young puppies and older dogs.

2. The great number of "unknown" injuries is due to the fact that many of these dogs have been adopted from shelters or other humane organizations and the cause of their injury was not clear when they arrived as strays. They are typically believed to be victims of abuse and/or neglect.

3. Females in this group outnumber males nearly two to one, especially in the abuse category. A possible reason for this fact, not yet proven, may be that many abusers (typically men) see their victims (women, children, and family pets) as weak and therefore easy to control and harm. The author theorizes that female dogs are at an even greater risk of being abused by such individuals than male dogs as they are of the "weaker sex" and nothing more than a dumb and defenseless animal.

4. Twenty-six percent of these dogs could be spared amputation with proper containment and/or supervision; forty-eight percent could be spared amputation if saved from the hands of an abuser or a neglectful and uncaring owner; and twenty-six percent would occur naturally or without direct intent regardless of the type of care the owner provided.

5. Based on this survey, amputations resulting from injuries or illnesses other than auto accidents and cancer account for forty percent of the total number of dogs each year who undergo this surgery.

Bailey (amputee) and friend, Dancer, share a moment together in their own special dog bedroom. What lucky and well-loved dogs!

Photo Cathy Watson

While amputations resulting from cancer and birth defects can affect dogs living in any type of home or environment, many of the *injuries* suffered by canine amputees occur in rather specific locales. Abandonment, neglect, and dog fighting can result in injuries commonly seen in urban areas. Hunting and trapping accidents and run-ins with farming equipment and barbed wire fences generally occur in rural areas of the country. Many auto related injuries, boating accidents, toxic exposure and poisoning, and injuries due to lawnmowers and chainsaws typically occur in suburban localities. Of course wanton acts of cruelty and abuse can and do occur anywhere. Each of these different human environments poses its own unique threat to our pets. Responsible dog owners will do everything within their power to keep their dog safe from these dangerous situations. To learn more about preventive measures, see "Chapter 9: Prevention, Still the Best Medicine".

Who are the owners of canine amputees? For the most part, they are very caring and loving individuals. They consider their pets part of the family; many love them as much as one of their own children or in place of children. They generally do not harbor any prejudices toward the handicapped or disabled; they are willing to pursue and provide the best medical care necessary for the animal. With the cost of a typical amputation surgery ranging from six hundred to several thousand dollars and the cost of subsequent care (radiation, chemotherapy, and nutrition) often ranging into the thousands as well, the majority of canine amputee owners comes from medium and higher income brackets. Most will spare no expense to ensure that their dog receives the very best medical care that they can afford.

Even dog owners who themselves work in the veterinary field may find that one of their own is suddenly a patient. Such was the case with veterinarian Dr. Suzanne DeStefano and her beloved grey-hound, Betsy. Betsy was afflicted with osteosarcoma in her right rear leg in 1997. Being a veterinarian, Suzanne had access to a host of veterinarians and specialists that the average dog owner would never be able to access. These friends and colleagues quickly became involved in Betsy's case. They were determined to save the dog's life and support Suzanne in every respect.

Betsy's afflicted limb was amputated and she underwent a series of chemotherapy treatments, doing extremely well and never exhibiting any adverse reactions from the drugs. Because her care providers knew that osteosarcoma is ultimately fatal in nearly all cases, Betsy's health was monitored closely by her veterinarian-owner, and chest x-rays were performed every few weeks to determine if the cancer had metastasized to her lungs, usually the primary site to which such cancer will spread. To those individuals who chastised Suzanne for her efforts to comfort and save "just a dog," she gave this response:

> *"Betsy is family. My dogs are the children I chose to have. I will be funding no lavish weddings or ivy league college tuitions. I can do without a fancy car and expensive vacations. What she (Betsy) gave me can not be assessed monetarily."*

Betsy remained healthy and happy and clear of any signs of metastasis for many months. Then sadly, and unexpectedly for all the professionals involved, the cancer spread not to Betsy's lungs but to her pelvis. Even with their limitless access to medicine and science, Betsy's owner and newfound friends were unable to save her. Her condition deteriorated rapidly. Left with no other humane alternatives, Dr. DeStefano said her final good-byes to Betsy in the familiar surroundings of her home, wrapped in her owner's loving arms, on December 10, 1997.

Of her brave dog's ordeal, Dr. DeStefano believes as most amputee owners do:

> *"I have never regretted pursuing her amputation and treatments. She had four glorious months that summer and fall where she walked on the boardwalk, ran the beach, ate ice cream, and sailed across Lake Winnipesaukee in her own little boat. She never cared about being three-legged. She cared about being alive and being with us."*

Unfortunately, not everyone can pursue costly medical procedures for their pets. Dog owners with limited incomes may not be able to elect amputation surgeries and traditional follow-up procedures for their dogs. Also, such individuals rarely have the resources to afford health insurance for their animals. In these cases, pet owners may find that their only affordable and humane option is euthanasia. Though this may not be what they prefer, their financial resources ultimately dictate the choices they must make. This can be a very guilt-ridden and traumatic decision for pet owners to make, and the veterinarian involved must be compassionate and understanding for clients finding themselves in such situations.

Of course, there are those individuals who simply abandon a pet in need of medical attention. While some neglectful owners will do this, worse still are animal owners who are abusive; some individuals may simply kill the wounded animal outright. Many abused, abandoned, and injured dogs find their way into American animal shelters every year. While some are euthanized, when feasible, certain facilities rescue, treat, foster, and care for canine amputees. Some of these dogs are already amputees when they arrive at the shelter, usually having been subjected to a traumatic incident that caused them to lose a limb. Other dogs, when they arrive, are in such dire need of medical care that the shelter arranges with local vets to have the damaged limb amputated. These dogs may become "spokes-dogs" or "poster-puppies" for the shelter and for the plight of other homeless and abused animals in general. It should come as no surprise that many of these normal, lovable dogs are adopted by kind-hearted new owners and given a second chance at a long and happy life.

Though many different types of people may own canine amputees, one fact is certain about the amputees themselves. They are loved and cherished by their owners to a degree uncommon among even average dog owners. There is just something endearing and touching about these brave animals that demands that those around them love them unequivocally and completely. It is all or nothing with an amputee, and they will not settle for anything less.

Dog owners faced with the prospects of owning an amputee will quickly find themselves in a very unique group, deeply influenced by their emotions regarding their pet's life. When faced with the decision of resigning their pet to a life on three legs, these people will be seized by an emotional roller coaster that will become the most difficult aspect of their ordeal to understand and with which to come to terms. Make no mistake, all owners faced with this scenario will experience an emotional upheaval. The decision they face is a simple and straightforward one—either amputate the affected limb and save or improve the animal's quality and quantity of life or euthanize. Period. There is no maze of choices to pick from. It is either do it or don't—that simple. Yet being the wonderfully complex beings that we are, humans will make this decision much more complicated and torturous than it needs to be. In order to be able to help our dogs, we must understand why we do this to ourselves.

Humans are creatures of habit. We live our lives according to consistent and familiar routines. When this routine is suddenly and unexpectedly altered, it creates havoc in our lives, causing us to become fearful, anxious, and uncertain. We find it hard to make decisions, or even to function, when faced with such stress. A dog owner whose pet is suddenly afflicted by a life-threatening injury or illness and requires surgery is experiencing just such a life-changing and routine-shattering occurrence. Under such circumstances, "normalcy" in our lives cannot be reinstated until we can gain control of the situation, which ultimately means getting a firm handle on our emotions.

The first emotions a dog owner will experience when his or her pet is injured—or a determination of cancer has been made—include shock, anger, guilt, and denial. Shock is a natural reaction to any unexpected and traumatic event. The normal routine has suddenly been shattered, and the person is taken unaware. Humans' fragile equilibriums cannot shift gears so quickly, and so they reel from the quick turn of events. Shock can effect people not only emotionally, making brains hurt and hearts ache, but even physically, causing nausea or illness. This is quite normal. The terrible out-of-control feeling will pass or begin to fade as the owner switches tracks and comes to grips with the situation.

As the initial shock passes, some dog owners may experience anger or outrage at the person they feel is responsible for the animal's predicament. This may be the car driver who hit the dog when it ran out into the street or the veterinarian who did not feel that tiny lump at the dog's last physical exam. Owners may verbalize their pain against those they feel have wronged them. More likely they will internalize their anguish and allow the anger to brew and churn within. These are all natural, human reactions. It is instinctive to want to lash out when we have been wounded. Having someone or something to be angry at allows us an outlet for our emotions; it gives us something to do. Of course, blindly and impulsively acting out because of our emotions can land us in hot water—or even in jail. Hopefully the influences of society and our own moral corner-stones will encourage us to exercise restraint and self-control when we are under the influence of such powerful emotions. Our anger should be harnessed to give us strength for what lies ahead and not allowed to go galloping off in all directions.

Anger is usually followed closely by guilt. When we have expended our anger against others, we redirect it toward ourselves. "It is my fault," we tell ourselves. "I allowed this to happen." Sadly, in some ways, we are correct. As the animal's keeper, it is our responsibility to keep the animal safe and healthy. If we fail in this duty by allow-ing our pet to run loose or ignoring changes in our pet's state of health, we really do not have anyone to blame but ourselves when something bad happens. However, even with careful vigilance, acci-dents and illnesses still occur. We cannot prevent or guard against every inevitability. Ultimately, guilt should act as a hard lesson learned. It teaches us to change old habits and ways of thinking and not to make the same mistakes twice.

Denial may present itself if we have not recovered from the initial impact of the pet's ordeal. Denial is our mind's inability to absorb and process the shock. Instead of moving through the natural phases of anger and guilt, we jump passed them or avoid them alto-gether by denying reality. "The vet got it wrong," our mind whispers. "My dog's not sick. Perhaps the lab results got mixed up. Perhaps it was someone else's dog that got hit, not mine. Perhaps they are wrong." Perhaps, perhaps, perhaps...

But once faced with hard evidence, denial will fade so that we can begin to comprehend and process what has happened and start to make decisions about what we now must do. Human beings are, after all, doers. We do not like to be helpless. We have a burning desire to take action and become involved in change once we acknowledge it. Change is the ultimate driving force behind our survival. Without it we would surely stagnate and die. Change keeps us sharp, makes us learn, encourages us to become more than we were a second ago. But how does one prepare to face the change an amputation will cause? After regaining some control over initial emotions, how does the pet owner determine which is the best course of action to take for the pet and for his or herself? How does he or she deal with the new emotions that will surely follow?

As the decision to amputate or not becomes of paramount importance and the time for making a decision grows shorter, average dog owners often feel confused, alone, uncertain, and helpless about what the decision should be. These feelings generally arise from the fact that they have no experience in these matters, no one they know has any experience, and the answers to their many questions are elusive. Like so many others, Kim Standley of Texas was faced with these many unknowns when informed that her twelve-year-old Doberman, Euro, was suffering from osteosarcoma.

> *"The hardest thing for us was not knowing what to expect when going through the amputation. We looked for all the information we could find. We wanted to not only know what he would be like in a couple of months, but what the first few days and weeks would be like and how he would look."*

Because humans have a strong desire to understand things, to know "why," we look to examples from others and to reports from history to help us make informed decisions. When we are faced with a lack of information, it can be very frustrating and frightening. Trying to understand what it will mean to own a canine amputee and what can be expected for that dog's life are unknowns that have never been properly addressed by any experienced and authoritative figure in the pet care industry. Even veterinarians, those who perform the actual surgery, have not been able to alleviate fears or offer sound advice, recommendations, or helpful anecdotes to help pet owners to make decisions. Hopefully, the reader will find enlightenment within these pages. This book should be a starting place for you to find the answers you are seeking.

What is cancer? Why did my dog get it? How will my dog look or act after the surgery? How will he get around? Is my dog a good candidate for amputation? If not, why not? Will he have a good life? *Should I amputate?* This book attempts to answer these questions by offering sound advice, hard facts, and the personal experiences of those who have been where you are now. By providing this information, we trust that you can find hope, inspiration, and strength to make the decisions that you need to make quickly and with assurance and resolve.

"Molly"   *Photo Fred & Rebecca Dolloff*

"I believe that he does better on three legs,
than I do on two. The vet says
he doesn't realize he only has three!"

Natalie & Bud Hodgen

Chapter 2

The History of Amputation

"Serena"   *Photo Fran Pinto*

With the exception of assisted childbirth, amputation may be the oldest form of medical surgery, for humans as well as animals. Though we will never know for certain, it may be that amputation predates all other forms of medical intervention. Perhaps even our crude Neanderthal cousins knew of the life-saving benefits of such drastic action. Certainly our ancient ancestors would have been exposed to a myriad of debilitating and life-threatening circumstances in which amputation may have been the only logical solution. With nothing but the most basic stone tools at their disposal, it would be an understatement to say that the surgery itself was often as terrible as the affliction. One has to wonder whether the ancients practiced this crude but effective medical treatment.

Prior to the development of "modern" medicine, the only sure way to save the life of a person whose limb was badly injured or diseased was to remove it. Of course, human nature being what it is, not all amputations were intended as therapeutic treatments. Some human amputations in ancient times were employed as forms of punishment. In many societies, the common punishment for thievery was to remove one or both hands of the criminal—a very convincing deterrent, indeed. In other cultures, an adulterous woman might have her nose amputated as a punishment and constant reminder of her indiscretion. Surviving these early surgeries was a miracle, due not only to the risk of bleeding to death, but also of succumbing to catastrophic infection.

While early man might lose a limb in the daily routine of his difficult and often dangerous existence, the greatest use of amputation, by far, was during times of war. Throughout history, with few or no medical supplies available on the battlefield, and even less time to deal with overwhelming numbers of badly wounded soldiers, amputation became the quick fix to save a man's life and get him back to work. If the individual was no longer suitable for battle, then at least he would live to pay taxes to the state. Half a taxpayer was better than no taxpayer at all. These hasty, battlefield surgeries were of the crudest form. There was no anesthesia; sterilizing of surgical instruments was unheard of; wound care consisted of cauterizing the open stump with a firebrand. As history marched along, medical knowledge, like everything else, advanced as well. Thank goodness!

During the Renaissance Period, a French surgeon, Ambriose Pare, developed a method of amputation by means of forceps and ligature, instead of the standard practice of stanching bleeding by means of fire. In the late 1800s, a German surgeon, Johannes Friedrick August von Esmarch, invented a method for keeping the limb nearly bloodless during surgery. His inspiration for such work? He was a military surgeon. It was with small steps such as these that the practice of amputation on humans slowly improved.

Where animals are concerned, amputation in some form or another is also a very ancient practice. Castration and polling are perhaps the only animal surgeries that predate it. Docking, the removal or amputation of a portion of a tail, was undoubtedly first practiced on domestic herds of sheep. Removal of the sheep's naturally long tail would have made birthing easier and would have kept the animal cleaner—both important incentives when one considers the lack of medical treatments for sick or unhealthy livestock back then and the great abundance of predators eager to make off with a diseased or overly odiferous animal. Even today, many farmers still use the simple and foolproof method of tying a ligature around the tail of a lamb until the dead, lower portion simply falls off. This is amputation in its most basic form.

A close runner-up to amputations on domestic sheep would have been those for early man's most important companion and ally— the dog. No animal in history has been more surgically altered and manipulated than the dog. The history of such alterations (amputations) arose as a matter of need, pure and simple. Ancient canines actually served important purposes in the early days of their relationships with humans, and serious injuries were no doubt commonplace. Dogs were not kept as pampered pets. Early man's canine counterparts were expected to hunt and herd and otherwise earn their keep. It became common practice to remove the overly long tails, earflaps, or dewclaws of working dogs. These appendages could easily snag and tear while the dog worked in thick brush and rough country or could be damaged in an encounter with an adversary such as a wolf or bear. Such injuries could cause the dog not only a great deal of pain, but could threaten its very existence. Infection was always a serious risk, but, more importantly, a dog that could no longer perform its duties for its master was useless and would quickly be destroyed. There was little compassion or tolerance for animals that could not earn their keep.

In Anglo-Saxon England in the Middle Ages, exhibitions of bull and bear baiting and dog fighting became popular events. Owners of these fighting dogs learned quickly that the dog with the shortest ears and tails provided the opponent with the fewest possible grips. The animal not easily held and pinned most often emerged victorious. Amputating a dog's ears and tail became commonplace among the sporting crowd.

Also around this time in England, an interesting and cruel amputation custom arose, enforced by local law. All villages of the period were required to keep a number of mastiffs for the purpose of protecting the king's deer from predation by wolves, bears, wildcats, and poachers. While this would seem a noble calling for any animal, the law in fact contained an ironic twist. The king's representative, known as the "Regarder," was entrusted with the duty of "gauging" the mastiffs of the local communities. He possessed a measuring gauge and was required to examine each dog in the village. If the mastiff was small enough to squeeze through the gauge, then he or she was not considered a threat to the king's deer. If the dog was too large to fit through the gauge, then he or she could possibly be as much a threat to the royal herds as the predators he or she was supposed to guard against. The solution to controlling these large dogs was to remove three toes of a front foot by means of a hammer and chisel. It was believed that this would ensure that the dog could not "course" the king's quarry. No doubt it simply precipitated the demise of the animal. Since dogs only possess four toes on each foot, the removal of three toes on such a large beast would render the animal useless, unable to perform any duty whatsoever. This became a sad but effective means to control not only the dog population, but also the peasant population as well, ensuring that no poor soul with a big dog might presume to illegally hunt the king's deer to feed his starving family. This is the only historical instance the author has found in which canine amputations were performed not for a clearly beneficial purpose but for no other reason than greed and conceit.

As particular breeds of dog became established in different countries, each designed and bred to perform specific tasks and duties, the manner in which their ears and tails should be cropped became established as well. These alterations, though arising as a matter of need and common sense, also became the criteria by which certain breeds later were recognized and distinguished. Traditions were established. Even today, many years after the dog's true usefulness has been all but forgotten and abandoned, we still honor the heritage of these individual breeds by having licensed veterinarians perform the necessary cropping and dockings according to each breed's standard. Some countries, riding the wave of animal rights activism, have now outlawed breed specific ear and tail alterations. The heritage of many breeds has suddenly been tossed out the window, dooming such breeds to the fate of mongrelization, or, at the very least, politically correct mediocrity. With all of modern society's medical advances, it would make far more sense (in this author's opinion) to require the administration of proper anesthesia or pain control techniques, as is done with spaying and neutering procedures, and to allow dog breeders and owners to choose to honor their particular breed's heritage if they so wish. In the end, only history will tell whether we have made the right decisions to abandon this wealth of canine tradition by prohibiting surgical alterations.

"Prince Toby Orry" (1916) a three-legged hound whose image graced many tourist items prior to WWI. He was touted as the only living representative of the Manx Coat of Arms.

Photo Mary Thurston, Copyright Animalimage.com

For hundreds of years, canine amputees have held unique status on the Isle of Man. Legend has it that King Alexander III, whose Scottish rule during 1266 A.D. included the now-British Isle of Man, was so fascinated by a three-legged dog race held on that island that he adopted a three-legged design as the official crest for the land. (In reality, the design was most likely a very ancient sun symbol used by local tribes.) Today the design is now the national symbol of the Isle of Man (see next page). It appears on all of the island's flags and currency and on some of its coins and postage stamps. On July 12, 1996, Her Majesty made official the granting of the Coat of Arms of the Isle of Man. This coat of arms depicts the traditional three legs on a field of red, surmounted by a crown and flanked by a falcon and a crow. Beneath the design is the motto: "*Quocunque Jeceris Stabit,*" which translates as "Whithersoever you throw it, it will stand." Could there be a more fitting motto for canine amputees everywhere?

Throughout antiquity, limb amputations for dogs were much rarer than for humans. While a catastrophic injury might end the usefulness of a dog, so might a limb amputation, even if it saved the animal's life. As has already been mentioned, dogs of old lived very hard, purposeful lives. They were expected to contribute to the

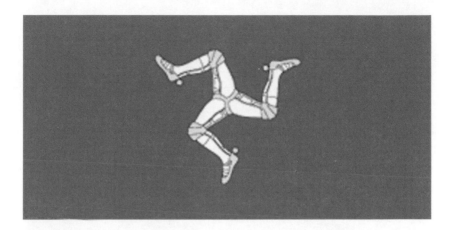

livelihood of the owner. Even if the owner believed that his dog could return to work with only three legs and perform his duties as before, the time that the dog might need to recover and the amount of care necessary to heal would negate any benefit that might be attained from such a risky procedure. Severely diseased or injured animals were often culled from the pack as a matter of simple economics. Throughout most of time, the poor and middle class found it excruciatingly hard to provide for themselves and their families. Providing time and sustenance for a useless dog would have been unimaginable.

Of course, there were no doubt exceptions to this fact. For those dogs lucky enough to have been owned by the rich or nobility, things may have been quite different. It is not unreasonable to think that some caring nobleman or woman, unable to bear the thought of living without a trusted hunting companion or beloved lapdog, would have pursued any attempt to save the animal's life. But these fortunate "pets" would have been the exception in days gone by.

Perhaps the most noted royal individual of modern times to own a canine amputee is Queen Elizabeth. On her eighteenth birthday, Princess Elizabeth was given a Pembroke corgi named Susan. The breed became a favorite of the Queen, who has had ten generations of corgis bred from Susan, including one that was a canine amputee.

Today in most civilized countries throughout the world, dogs are no longer considered working animals or livestock. They have become pampered pets, extensions of the trappings of our everyday lives. They are companions, family members, even surrogate children to many. The species as a whole is loved, protected, and cared for by its human caretakers unlike any other animal in recorded history. For years, marketing and research firms in the United States have reported that Americans spend more money annually on their pets than they do on their children. Perhaps this is simply a way of repaying a debt long overdue for everything the canine race has done for us.

BUCKINGHAM PALACE

27th March, 2000

Dear Miss Neal

I am writing to thank you for your letter in which you enquire about one of The Queen's dogs which had a leg amputated some years ago.

I am afraid it is not possible to send you detailed information concerning this, or to supply you with photographs, but I am able to confirm that the dog enjoyed a very active life after the operation.

Yours Sincerely

Philippa de Pass

Lady-in-Waiting

Miss S. Neal

In 1974, Girl's amputation cost $50. Today this surgery can cost several hundred—even several thousand—dollars.

Photo Maxine Jaffee

With this new mentality toward the keeping of pets and the tremendous change in the economic and financial resources of the majority of the American population, animal health care has become of paramount importance to dog owners. Amputation, once a rare and risky procedure for a mere dog, has become commonplace. The surgery itself has come a long way from the crude fumblings of our ancestors. Though a serious operation, limb amputation has become fairly routine, with the majority of surgeries being performed by general practitioners—the neighborhood dog and cat vet. Only very complicated surgeries, or those requiring complex treatments such as for cancer, are performed by veterinary specialists at large veterinary universities.

Nowadays, most general veterinarians do not find it odd to perform several amputation surgeries per year. These numbers increase for vets located in farm and rural areas where dogs are exposed to greater risks of injury from a variety of sources. The increasing incidence of cancer among dogs (638,000+ cases per year in this country alone) has almost ensured that the regular veterinarian will be called upon several times a year to perform life-saving amputations on some of his or her regular clients.

On average, the veterinary teaching hospital performs about thirteen limb amputations per year. (The reported statistics ranged from four per year to nearly thirty, with thirteen being about average.) There are twenty-seven veterinary colleges in this country. About four hundred limb amputations are performed each year at veterinary colleges across this country. The number of limb amputations performed by general practitioners far exceeds the number performed by the specialists. The American Veterinary Medical Association reported in 1994 that of the more than fifty-five thousand professionally active veterinarians in the United States, approximately 39,600 are engaged in the treatment of small animals (dogs and cats). If every one of these vets performed only one emergency amputation per year (certainly not unthinkable in this day and age), it would generate approximately thirty-nine thousand canine limb amputations. Through surveys the author conducted on a small population and by her painstaking interpretation of this information, the author has determined that 37,200 dogs in this country require limb amputations every year—very close in keeping with the generalized assumption above. Clearly, these amounts indicate an unprecedented modern, medical response to serious disease or catastrophic injury in our canine companions. It is certainly a subject worthy of further study. Unfortunately, no organization in this country has ever attempted to compile and process any data pertaining to canine amputees. Until recently, no one compiled accurate records on the number of dogs afflicted with cancer each year, either. In 1999, the Morris Animal Foundation approved the funding of a scientific study to be conducted by the Armed Forces Institute of Pathology, under the direction of Dr. Michael Peterson. This study, entitled "Feasibility Study: Developing a Population-Based Prospective Canine Cancer Registry" will attempt to develop a system for collecting and analyzing data regarding the types and frequencies of cancers affecting the United States population of canines. It is hoped that this information may then be useful in preventing, treating, and controlling the wildfire spread of canine cancers. For more information on this program, you can contact the Morris Animal Foundation at www.morrisanimalfoundation.org and refer to study #97PT-16.

Chapter 3
Canine Amputations—
Terminology and Criteria

"Jack"   *Photo Ann Thompson*

We have learned that amputation has taken a long and perilous road throughout the course of human and canine history. We are grateful that it is available to our animals and us as a treatment option for many ailments that afflict both species. As stated earlier in this book, as responsible dog owners, we must always be conscious of that one inescapable fact: *any dog, any where, at any time, for any reason can become an amputee.* For this reason alone, it would be beneficial for all dog owners to learn as much as they can about the disability and about the diseases and injuries that require amputation. This chapter will examine some of the specifics about the condition itself and attempt to provide a clearer explanation of certain phrases and terminology.

Congenital amputee "Ariel," a Saluki, was born with only half of her right front limb. An amputation removed the useless stump.
Photo courtesy Carrie Haggert

Amputation is defined as the removal of a body part, especially by surgery. An *amputee* is defined as one who has had one or more limbs removed by means of amputation. We will learn in later chapters that amputees are not only the result of medical surgery. *Congenital amputees* result when a child or animal is born with missing or incomplete extremities. Most canine congenital amputees are culled at birth. Professional breeders generally opt to have the animal painlessly euthanized. They know that it is very difficult for such puppies to find loving homes. For such a genetic blunder to occur in their breeding program—well, suffice it to say,

Here we see an example of a severe birth defect. This German shepherd, "Chawla," was born without both front legs. While dogs manage very nicely on only three legs, this puppy will be hard pressed to enjoy a normal life with such a disability.

Photo courtesy Carrie Haggert

it is not something they want to be widely known among their peers. One can only hope that the dogs used in that breeding would never be bred to each other again and that the entire breeding line and program would be seriously reevaluated.

In a case where a canine congenital amputee with an in- complete, deformed, or non-functional limb is allowed to live, surgery to fully remove the limb may be recommended. If the animal attempts to use the limb as it does its three normal legs, the dog may seriously injure the incomplete limb, which could lead to massive infection and complications. Generally, incomplete limbs are not protected by the thick, calloused pads of the normal canine foot, and the thinner skin covering the partial limb can be torn, bruised, or worn away. Conscientious veterinarians will recommend amputation to their clients for the well being of the animal.

When a limb is completely removed—right up to and including the entire hip or shoulder—it is commonly known as a *complete disarticulation*. The portion of a limb allowed to remain following a partial or modified amputation is known as a *stump*.

Amputation is unique among the disabilities experienced by domestic dogs. Unlike deafness and blindness, which typically occur gradually over time as a result of the aging process or a bit more suddenly as the direct and ultimate end result of the progression of a disease, a limb amputation is never a *direct* product or end result of either age or disease but is instead a curative or palliative procedure to address and/or remove a disease. (The only exception to this is in the case of a congenital amputee, when the puppy is born with a missing limb. However, congenital amputees are almost a unique class unto themselves, and these cases are very rare.) Furthermore, unlike the other major canine disabilities (deafness and blindness) there is generally no measurable diminishment of the dog's quality of life. Most amputees can continue to work, play, and enjoy life just as they did prior to their surgery, whereas the majority of dogs who have lost their vision or hearing can no longer engage in many of the activities they once did before their impairment. Also, there is usually no behavioral change for an amputee once fully recovered from the surgery. They maintain their normal moods and behaviors, whereas dogs suffering from blindness or deafness can become fearful, confused, depressed, or snappy as a result of the new stresses that their condition has imposed on them. For all amputees, the injury, disease, or genetic abnormality experienced by the dog is the direct cause of their disability; amputation is simply a remedy to treat the cause. By removing the limb, the cause (the disease or injury) is removed, and normal behavior and activity generally resume in an amazingly short time. So, while amputation is considered by most to be a disability, it is also very often the treatment for curing the dog of what ails it and allowing it to resume a normal life.

Diseases and injuries for which amputation is commonly employed as a cure can be classified into two very distinct groups. They are:

cancer-related circumstances and *non-cancer-related circumstances.* While dogs in either group will typically undergo the same basic surgical procedure, it is imperative to divide amputations into these two distinct classifications due to the very different events that precede and follow the surgery. A dog who has undergone amputation in response to a cancer threat is a wholly unique individual from one who has undergone the same type of surgery due to an auto accident or birth defect. For the canine amputee resulting from an accident, the changes brought on by the amputation itself are generally the only concerns of the owner. For a dog who has been diagnosed with cancer and who has undergone amputation in order to save or extend its life, the amputation is secondary and almost inconsequential. It is the cancer that is the primary focus for that animal, his owners, and his health care providers. Both of these classifications will be examined separately and in greater detail in Chapters 4 and 5.

Amputations are performed for one or more of the following reasons:

- Palliative
- Disease removal
- Emergency or life-threatening cause
- Cosmetic or appearance
- Financial

Palliative amputations are generally performed in situations where the dog has suffered extensive soft tissue damage from a traumatic injury, and the healing process has ended, but the animal has not regained the control or use of the limb. The limb is now simply a dead appendage and provides no useful function. Many dogs will "worry" such a limb, biting and licking at it constantly, even causing severe damage to themselves due to the lack of feeling in the limb. This type of behavior was evidenced by Elliot, a golden retreiver owned by Sarah Ramsay. The dog had been hit by a car and suffered a severe rotator cuff injury. Though she recovered from the ordeal, she never regained use of the limb. After two occasions in which

A severe fracture of this puppy's left hind limb required amputation. "Bodger"
Photo courtesy Anita Yusko

Elliot attempted to chew off her own leg, it was decided to surgically remove the limb to comfort her. It worked, and Elliot has lived a happy, contented life as an amputee ever since.

Disease removal amputations are pretty straightforward. They are performed to remove a disease, or as much of it as possible, in order to save the dog's life. Cancer comes to mind most readily but other diseases such as gangrene or catastrophic infection also create candidates for limb removal. In some instances, the disease can be completely eliminated through amputation. In the majority of cases, though, amputation provides for an extension of life but does not halt the spread of the disease completely, and the dog eventually succumbs to the disease or complications thereof.

Amputations required due to ***life-threatening situations*** include such things as severe frostbite, crushing, irreparable compound fracture, and gunshot wounds. This type of amputation is performed when there is little hope of repairing the damage by any other means and as a means to deter spreading infection or other complications. Most cancer amputations are performed to attempt to remove disease and slow or alter a life-threatening condition.

"Elliot"   *Photo by author*

Cosmetic amputations are those generally performed to improve
the appearance or the movement and mobility of the dog. A dog
with a severe birth defect or one that has been the object of abuse
might be an appropriate candidate for this type of surgery. Such was
the case of Spikey, a young boxer male. Spikey had been terribly
neglected by his first owner, who never sought treatment for the
puppy when he was hit by a car. His fractured front leg shriveled
grotesquely up against his body, and the nails grew right into the
pads of his foot. To make matters worse, he had buckshot imbedded
in his face and back, and a portion of bone protruded from his
poorly docked tail. This poor dog was lucky to have been saved
from certain death by a dedicated boxer rescue person, Jo Monten,
who had Spikey's deformed and useless leg amputated and also saw
to his other injuries. He was then placed in the home of Diana Lynn
Stout, his devoted and loving owner for the past five years. Without
undergoing amputation, it is questionable whether Spikey would
ever have found a new home. As much as we may try to deny it,
some humans can be very superficial, and appearances are important to them. A dog in as rough a state as Spikey was when rescued
would have found it hard, indeed, to find a good and caring home.

Spikey and mom enjoying a cuddle.   *Photo courtesy Diana Stout*

This situation clearly illustrates that a clean, neat amputation can leave the dog far more appealing than if allowed to continue with a deformity. The operation would have also alleviated any chronic pain the poor animal had been experiencing since the initial accident.

A deformed, useless, and lifeless limb will not be missed by a dog. In a very short time, a loving owner will not miss it, either. One must realize that these deformed extremities, if not removed, can create problems for the animal other than pain and discomfort. They can become entangled in bedding or shrubbery or, even worse, hooked in the collar of a playmate, endangering the welfare of both animals.

Financial. Human economics play a large role in the treatment of companion animals. With the cost of pet health care rising five times faster than human health care, this is a major consideration for most owners. Pet health insurance has become available during the past few years to cover a variety of ailments, but those animals covered by health insurance—barely one percent of the pet population, according to the American Society for the Prevention of Cruelty to Animals—are usually the exception rather than the rule. Most pet owners are not even aware that such coverage exists. In cases where financial limitations on the part of the owner may prevent him or her from being able to authorize expensive but necessary treatments—such as femoral head replacements for severely dysplastic animals or the repairs of complicated leg fractures—amputation is often an acceptable alternative to euthanasia. To find affordable health insurance coverage for your pet, see "Insurance Companies" in the Directory section at the end of this book.

Small breeds, such as terrier, make very good amputee candidates. "Stumpett"
Photo courtesy Peggy Metcalf

Regardless of the illness or injury a dog has sustained, he or she must meet a specific set of criteria in order to be a good candidate for amputation surgery. Though now routine, this is still a major operation and should never be considered lightly. In making a recommendation to the owner that his pet should undergo amputation, a veterinarian must consider the following criteria:

1. *Age, weight, and breed of dog. These are the most important items to consider when first evaluating a patient for amput*ation surgery. An older, obese large- or giant-breed dog will typically not fare as well as a younger, leaner, smaller breed. In fact, based on age, weight, and breed alone, a veterinarian may make a recommendation against amputation. Elderly animals are prone to greater complications, longer recovery times, and increased difficulty learning new

skills than younger ones. Overweight dogs will have problems not experienced by their leaner counterparts, such as increased fatigue and discomfort from carrying a heavy body mass on three legs as opposed to four, and they are at greater risk of overexertion or injury, such as a torn cruciate ligament or back trauma. *Breed of dog* generally relates to both age and weight. A giant breed of dog that is known to have a life span of only eight or nine years may not be a good candidate for amputation if brought in at age eight and one-half. The chances that the animal will succumb shortly to age-related complications nearly ensures that he will reap no benefit from the surgery. Also, a heavy breed of dog, such as a Newfoundland or Saint Bernard, may find being an amputee so difficult, because of his great mass, that the surgery provides no benefits to him either. On the other hand, a young, athletic, small, female Newfie might be an ideal candidate for amputation, while the elderly, overweight pug is not. The veterinarian must consider each case individually based on age, weight, and breed before considering any other criteria. Should the dog be deemed an acceptable risk based on these three items, then further examination of the client's condition and lifestyle can be considered.

2. *Temperament of the Animal. It is impor*tant for the vet to consider the dog's temperament prior to recommending surgery. Just as with humans, each canine personality type may handle amputation differently. A very high-strung, nervous animal with a very low pain tolerance will not respond to the surgery and the reality of being an amputee as well as would a settled, gentle, tolerant animal with a high threshold for pain. Another behavioral trait to consider is the aggressive or dominant animal. This trait may worsen following surgery due to pain, apprehension, or a feeling that dominance is being threatened, making this animal all but impossible to treat or live with. The behavior of the animal must be given careful consideration before proceeding further.

3. *Attitude of the Owner.* Many animals who are excellent candidates for amputation are owned by individuals who cannot deal

with any type of disfigurement, and so for them amputation is simply not an option. These people generally decide to have their pet put to sleep. It is unfortunate that a human's aversions must be used as criteria in determining the course of treatment for a sick or injured animal, but it must. For some people, owning a disabled dog is an indication—they feel—that they are not perfect, that there is something wrong with them, and that society will hold it against them. For others, there is an underlying prejudice against those they view as *cripples*. Rather than viewing amputation as life saving, they may view it as disfigurement that they would never permit their dog to undergo. It is not difficult to understand why some people in society may feel this way when one considers that throughout much of modern history, our primary exposure to amputees has been in the form of villains such as Captain Ahab, Captain Hook, Peg-Leg Pete, or Long John Silver.

Another important aspect to consider regarding the owner involves not the attitude so much as the physical health of that person. For instance, an elderly client who owns a mastiff in need of amputation may not be able to physically care for the animal as required following the surgery. Many dogs initially need to be lifted, or assisted, in and out of vehicles and up and down stairs. An elderly or infirm individual may not be able to perform such tasks, making the viability of owning or caring for a canine amputee impossible. The owner must be willing *and* able to care for a disabled pet.

4. *Front-leg vs. rear-leg amputation.* Seventy-five percent of a dog's weight is supported by its front legs, an important consideration when evaluating the canine patient. Consideration is especially important when evaluating the large or giant breeds that may find it very difficult to maneuver as a front-leg amputee. For these breeds, a rear-leg amputation is generally more feasible and easier for the animal to adapt to physically. Following amputation, a dog ambulates in a type of "hopping" gait, as opposed to a normal, reaching gait in the non-amputee. A dog missing a front leg must throw back his/her head, neck, and upper body (shoulders and withers) to

release weight from the front-end assembly in order to take a step with the one front leg. This requires a great deal of effort and energy and can understandably become very tiring for large dogs. On the other hand, a rear-leg amputee simply compresses his back and gives a little hop behind to bring the one rear leg into play. Because there is far less weight on this end of the body, this mode of travel is much simpler and requires far less expenditure of effort or energy. Thus for large dogs, a rear-leg amputation is preferable though not a necessity. All dogs learn to adapt, and most handle the new method for movement quite well once they get the hang of it, regardless of whether they are missing a front or rear leg. They should, however, be kept lean and not allowed to gain excess weight in order to keep the load-lifting requirements on that front end as low as possible. Small dogs, because of their lighter body mass, generally make no distinction between a front or rear amputation. They handle both types equally well.

5. *Current Medical Problems.* The overall health condition of the animal must be thoroughly examined prior to amputation. A dog that has been diagnosed with such an advanced case of cancer that his life expectancy is only a few weeks is not an appropriate candidate for amputation. He may not even fully recover from the surgery itself before he succumbs to his disease. To put such an animal through this type of procedure would be cruel and meaningless and certainly not in the best interest of the animal. No conscientious vet will perform an amputation on such a terminally ill creature.

Chronic problems with the musculoskeletal system must also be considered. A dog already suffering from advanced hip dysplasia or arthritis will only worsen when weight is shifted onto an opposing, compromised limb. Traumatic injuries such as those that occur in auto accidents, falls from a height, or abuse can have multiple complications. The muscular, ligamental, and neurological health of the other limbs, as well as the spine and pelvis, must be examined and determined to be free of any damage. Occasionally, spinal or pelvic fractures are not readily apparent and can be overlooked. Performing an amputation in such a case will only compound the problems already faced by the dog. In such a situation, it may be necessary to stabilize the damaged limb, if possible, and allow the other damaged body part time to heal properly before performing the amputation.

Another important consideration in evaluating the overall health of the amputee-to-be is chronic debilitating complications that may arise from post-surgical treatments such as chemotherapy and radiation. Systemic disorders can occur that compromise organ function or metabolic health, and these things present their own set of complications that can affect the desired outcome of the animal's recovery. In these cases, the overall prognosis must be considered, not just the results of the amputation.

Hopefully, this chapter has given the reader a clearer understanding of amputation surgery, why and when it is recommended to pet owners, and why a veterinarian may even recommend against such a treatment. By being more informed about this procedure, pet owners are better prepared to make the necessary decisions regarding life and death situations that may arise during the course of their pets' lives. We all wish that such incidences might never make themselves known to us or our cherished pets, but it would be foolish to assume, as so many people do nowadays, that "It could never happen to me (or my dog)."

Chapter 4
The Cancer Patient As Amputee

"Yapper"　　　　　　　　　*Photo Fran Pinto*

The owner of a dog that has been diagnosed with malignant cancer in a limb has much more to contend with than simply the concern of living with a canine amputee. In such a case, amputation is the least of the problems that he or she will encounter. The cancer itself is the most serious and devastating complication of such a condition. However, many owners can become consumed with uncertainties regarding how their dog will look or act as an amputee. Instead they should focus their attention on the real problem, the cancer. It is of utmost importance that the owner understands the nature of this life-threatening disease.

What exactly is cancer? In its simplest form, cancer is a condition that arises when a cell's genetic instructions go horribly awry. Every single cell in the body possesses a unique set of blueprints that tells that cell how to behave, what to do, and when to do it. Because of these instructions, the cell knows how and when to multiply and divide and when to stop or die. If these instructions become damaged in some way, the cell no longer behaves as it should. It may misinterpret its blueprint or abandon it altogether. This error within the cell's instructions can be caused by a genetic alteration or by direct damage. Believe it or not, every living thing—humans and pets included—has cancer cells inside its body at any given time. Normal bodily functions generally ensure that cancer cells are killed or discarded. Usually, when a cell becomes damaged, it simply dies, or the body's defenses spring into action to destroy it. When the body does not take action against cancerous cells, they can multiply at an alarming rate and divide out of all proportion to their original genetic instructions. Left unchecked, these vagrant cells can quickly multiply into a *tumor.*

Cancer tumors are typically classified into two categories: benign and malignant. A *benign* tumor is one that does not "invade" other surrounding tissues as it develops. It stays central to itself and usually presents a low health risk. A benign tumor can be something as familiar to us as a mole, birthmark, or fatty lump beneath the skin. These fatty lumps are usually called lipomas. If you pinch them with your fingers, they may feel like a tiny marble rolling around within the skin. There is generally no cause for alarm with this type of cyst unless it seems to be attached to tissue beneath the skin. It is always wise to have any unusual lumps or bumps examined by a veterinarian.

Malignant tumors, on the other hand, are quite another story. They grow and spread quickly, sending out roots and invading surrounding tissue, organs, and bones. As cells break off from these growths, they travel throughout the body by way of the bloodstream or lymph system and can create new tumor sites, independent from the original. This process of spread is known as a *metastasis*, and the cancer is said to be *metastatic*.

How do a cell's special instructions become damaged in the first place? There are several ways this can occur. Damage can be the result of a genetic defect. Every cell in the body contains paired chromosomes, thirty-eight in the dog compared to only twenty-three in humans. Upon these chromosomes are millions of genes, which contain the actual messages that the cell must interpret and act upon. They contain messages regarding the release of stomach acids, hair growth, and skin color, to name just a few. Because of the incredible number of genes involved, every time a cell divides, there is a chance that something may go wrong. The cell may then begin to operate with a set of instructions contrary to its original design. When this occurs, the cancer is said to be *genetically influenced*. When there is a known familial incidence among related individuals for a presentation of the same disease due to this type of genetic defect, the cancer is termed *hereditary*. The defect may be passed from one generation to the next.

There is also a chance for mutations to occur and go unchecked in an immune system that is severely weakened or damaged. In such cases, the body's natural defenses are unable to rally an offensive against the invading/mutating cells, and they are allowed to operate freely within the weakened host. Sick, young, or geriatric dogs are especially at risk to this type of cell damage, because their immune systems are not prepared or equipped to fight such a tremendous battle. Cancer that arises in this manner is considered to be an *immune-deficiency disease.*

There are also a great number of external influences that can damage a cell, causing it to mutate. Science today is spending incredible amounts of time, money, and resources to identify these causes and create guidelines to avoid exposure to their damaging influence. Cancer triggered by external forces is said to be due to *environmental or chemical factors.*

Some of the most common cancer-influencing factors to which our dogs are exposed on a daily basis include:

- cigarette smoke

- radiation—x-rays, electrical , etc.

- poisons and toxins (fertilizers, pesticides, cleaners, etc.)

- infectious agents

- improper diets (deficiencies or excesses in vitamins, minerals, amino acids, fats)

- trauma or injury

It is interesting to note that in the last category, trauma, it is now believed that even a violent fracture could drastically alter the cells' genetic instructions at the site of the injury, resulting in the development of cancer—perhaps long after the initial injury has healed. In their book, *Managing the Veterinary Cancer Patient* (Veterinary Learning Systems, Inc.), Drs. Anthony Moore and Gregory Ogilvie state that "osteosarcoma has been associated with sites of healed fractures or internal-fixation devices, implying that chronic irritation may play a role in tumor development." Clearly, many items that we could consider mundane in our daily lives, can, in fact, pose considerable threats to our animals and us. When a dog is exposed to two or more of the cancer-causing agents listed above, the odds for risk multiply dramatically. To learn about ways to decrease your dog's exposure to these agents, see "Chapter 9: Prevention, Still the Best Medicine."

Today, cancer is the leading cause of disease and death among dogs. The University of Pennsylvania estimates that eleven hundred or more dogs in every one hundred thousand will develop some form of cancer each year. Taking into account that there are some fifty-eight million dogs in this country, one may be appalled to learn that some 638,000 dogs, or one percent of the entire canine population, will be stricken with cancer each year, and this number is growing dramatically. At one time, naturally occurring diseases, such as rabies and distemper, were the leading cause of death among the United State's domestic canine population. Advances in immunology have all but eliminated outbreaks of these diseases. However, our society's blind rush toward the discovery and use of new technological wonders has given us a whole new range of unpredictable agents that, alone or in combination, can drastically affect the health of our dogs and ourselves.

Dogs are susceptible to developing many of the same types of cancer to which humans are prone. The only reassuring bit of information to be garnered from this fact is that many types of treatments work equally well for dogs and humans. In many cases, human treatments have evolved due to testing done on dogs to determine the efficacy of particular drugs or protocols. Also, new treatments that have been found to assist the human patient may be transferable to canine treatment. When such personal and important data and findings can be shared and utilized by two such different species, it should remind us just what an incredible debt we owe to man's best friend. Without the dog's assistance and sacrifice, there is no doubt that human history would be quite different.

Owners should be aware of the warning signs that may indicate a dog is suffering from cancer. Early detection of the disease is very important in saving the life of the animal and can make a great difference in the types of treatments implemented and the successful responses to these treatments. Dog owners should watch for the following early warning signs:

- Any abnormal mole, wart, lump, bump, or swelling that lingers or continues to grow or sores that refuse to heal

- Unexplained weight loss, lethargy, loss of appetite, or other changes in behavior

- Lameness, stiffness, exercise intolerance, loss of stamina, pain when touched in a certain area

- Bleeding or discharge from the nose, mouth, or eyes

- Bad body odor or mouth odor

- Difficulty breathing, urinating, defecating, or ambulating

If the owner witnesses any of these symptoms, he or she should immediately contact the animal's veterinarian and make an appointment to have the dog thoroughly examined. It is strongly recommended that the owner make notes regarding the onset of symptoms, their duration and extent, and any other behavioral or physiological changes noted. Following are descriptions of the most common cancer conditions that require amputation in dogs.

Primary Bone Tumors

Osteosarcoma

This is the most prevalent form of cancer in dogs today. Colorado State University estimates that at least ten thousand dogs per year are afflicted with osteosarcoma in this country alone. Of this number, seventy-five percent will possess tumors arising in the *appendicular skeleton* (in the limbs), making them prime candidates for amputations. Osteosarcoma is believed to arise in the *medullary cavity* of the bones. This is the marrow-filled area of the shafts of the long bones. From this location, the cancer spreads outward, destroying the *bone cortex* (the outer layers) and the *periosteum* or protective covering or skin on the bone. Osteosarcoma is an extremely fast-moving, devastating, and completely fatal disease. It accounts for approximately eighty-one percent of all cancer amputee cases, according to this author's research.

Presentation of osteosarcoma is usually first noted as pain or lameness in a limb. The dog may exhibit a limp or wobble in his or her gait. This is especially noticeable at a trot. X-rays taken at the early onset of the disease may provide inconclusive results, as the tumor may still be too small to distinguish. Subsequent x-rays show progression of the tumor's growth. The animal may refuse to bear weight on the affected leg as pain increases and may drag or elevate the limb, ambulating on three legs only. As the cancer spreads, destroying more bone and invading tissue, it causes extreme pain and discomfort. An increasing mass may become noticeable beneath the skin. Bone fractures are common as the tumor grows. In dogs that have a very high pain threshold or who are not closely monitored on a daily basis by the owner, a broken leg may be the first indication of the disease. Something as mundane as a run across the yard or a jump off the sofa can cause a severe fracture at the site of a tumor or its related micro-fractures.

The bones of the leg most commonly affected by osteosarcoma are: the *distal radius*, the main weight-bearing bone of the forearm; the *proximal humerus*, the largest bone in the front-leg assembly; the *distal femur*, or thigh bone, the heaviest bone in the dog's body and the largest bone of the rear-leg assembly; and the *proximal tibia*, the bone in the rear leg that corresponds to the radius of the front leg.

There have been some generalizations noted about the kind of dog typically affected by osteosarcoma. The disease is most prevalent in large or giant breeds of dog such as Great Dane, Newfoundland, Mastiff, Rottweiler, and Golden Retriever. This is probably due to the extreme pressures and stresses put on the bones of these dogs during their rapid growth stages from puppyhood to maturity.

"Arapaho"
Large breeds, such as German shepherds, are most commonly affected by bone cancers.

Photo Karen Dugan

The forelimbs are more often affected than the rear limbs, which makes sense when one understands that the front legs bear seventy-five percent of the entire weight of the body. This makes them more susceptible to strain and injury. As for gender predilection, males and females seem to be equally affected. But the disease is generally thought of as being one of old age. The median age for development is roughly eight years.

Many people may not consider eight very old. But as the average life span for a large or giant breed is typically six to ten years, one can see why osteosarcoma is considered a disease of old age. Of course there are exceptions to these generalizations, and even young or small dogs may develop the disease.

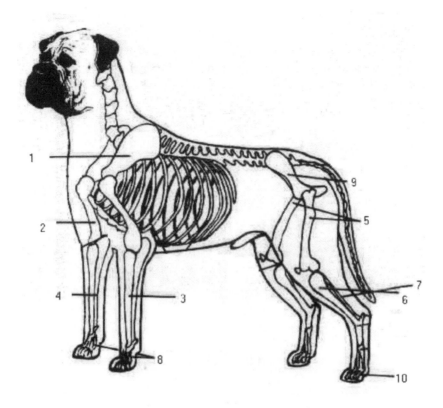

Bones of the limbs most commonly affected by cancer:

1) Scapula (shoulder)
2) Humerus (upper foreleg)
3) Ulna (lower foreleg)
4) Radius (lower foreleg)
5) Femur (upper thigh)
6) Tibia (lower thigh)
7) Fibula (lower thigh)
8) Metacarpals (pastern)
9) Pelvis
10) Phalanges (toes)

The prognosis for a dog afflicted with osteosarcoma is very poor. This type of cancer metastasizes aggressively throughout the body, especially to the vital organs such as the heart and lungs. Survival times are fairly short, regardless of the type of treatment sought. For a dog left untreated or treated by means of surgery alone (amputation), the survival time averages about six months, but may unfortunately be as short as a few weeks. Surgery done in combination with chemotherapy may extend the average survival time to more than a year. Newer, experimental types of treatment, such as hormone therapy, average only about seven months. There are, of course, exceptions to these averages, as there are to nearly every statement made regarding cancer. Some owners who have opted for amputation alone have seen their dogs survive and live relatively normal lives for more than one or two years. There have even been cases of complete *remission* reported. A remission is described as an abatement of a disease or a restoration to an original condition, as before the disease occurred. It may also mean a disappearance of all *detectable* evidence of cancer. In the case of osteosarcoma, remissions are extremely rare. It would be wrong to raise false hopes regarding the occurrences of these isolated "miracles," but we would be remiss not to mention that such wonders can, and do, occur. Bugsy, a golden retriever afflicted with osteosarcoma in his left rear leg, is an example of such a miracle. He experienced an amputation in 1993 to extend his life. His owner, Joyce Bagley, reports that to date the cancer has not metastasized, and Bugsy is enjoying a wonderful, pain-free life. The author's own dog, Izzy, is also an example of a complete remission. When Izzy underwent her amputation at the young age of two, her radiologists and pathologists confirmed that she was the victim of some type of bone cancer, possibly hemangiosarcoma, periosteal sarcoma, or even synovial sarcoma. Yet, six years later, at the age of eight (a ripe old age for any Bullmastiff, a breed for which the expected life span is only six to ten years), Izzy is still a lively, healthy, and vivacious dog with no complications whatsoever arising from her ordeal with cancer.

Of the other types of primary bone cancers not considered to be osteosarcoma, the following most commonly affect dogs.

Fibrosarcoma is a type of cancer that affects the connective tissues of the bone such as muscles and ligaments. It is fairly rare in the appendicular skeleton (limbs) and is seen much more frequently in the axial skeleton (of the trunk and head). Presentation of the disease is similar to osteosarcoma—indications of pain, lameness, or swelling. Dogs typically affected are older, with more likelihood for males over females. It has a slower rate of metastasis than osteosarcoma and survival rates following surgery and adjunctive treatment (chemo) range from about four to forty months.

Chondrosarcoma is a cancer arising in the cartilage of the bones. It is very rare to find it in the limbs; it typically affects the body of the animal. When it does target the limbs, it seems to affect the front legs more often than the rear and is considered a disease of the older dog. Survival rates based on amputation alone are somewhat better than for osteosarcoma, about eighteen months on average.

Hemangiosarcoma is a cancer arising primarily in the blood vessels. Like fibrosarcoma and chondrosarcoma, it is considered a fairly rare form of bone cancer. Unlike many other cancers, though, this one is seen mostly in *young* animals of the large or giant breed types. Because it is a vascular disease, cancerous cells spread quickly throughout the body, and there is an extremely high rate of metastasis. All the major organs—heart, liver, spleen, lungs—can be affected in a very short time. The survival rate is even poorer than for osteosarcoma—less than six months with amputation alone.

Periosteal sarcoma is a type of bone cancer that arises in the tough, fibrous membrane that surrounds the bone. This membranous sheeting does more than simply cover and protect the outside of the bone. It is also responsible for the formation of bone. (If a portion of periosteum is transplanted into muscle or other tissue, new bone begins to generate in those areas.) It also appears to be the agent that provides healing in the case of a broken bone. If the periosteum becomes detached from the bone, due to either disease or injury, the exposed bone will perish without it. Because the periosteum is a highly vascular tissue, cancer arising in this region can spread inward toward the bone and outward toward other tissues. Survival rates correspond to other types of primary bone tumors.

Primary Joint-Related Tumors

Synovial cell sarcoma originates in the synovial membrane of the joints. The membrane cushions the joints and produces synovial fluid to lubricate the joints. Though considered a very rare disease, it most frequently occurs in middle-aged (seven years old) male dogs of the larger breeds. It has a very low metastatic rate, and the survival time with amputation alone can be more than three years. Further treatment with a chemotherapeutic agent may offer an even longer period of freedom from the disease.

Secondary Tumors

Secondary tumors are those that spread from another "primary" site of development such as is commonly the case in lymphosarcoma, mammary, or prostate cancer, or various lung lesions. Treatment of secondary tumors by amputation is usually performed for palliative reasons only. Due to the advanced presence of cancer elsewhere in the body, limb removal for secondary tumors is never curative. It *may* help to extend the life of the animal but generally only serves to make the time remaining more comfortable. This in itself can be a very important priority for some pet owners who are concerned that their dog be spared as much pain and discomfort as possible until no further options or treatments remain.

Megan, a Bedlington Terrier, became an amputee as the result of a mast cell tumor. Her cancer and subsequent surgery did not diminish her quality or quantity of life.
Photo Sheryl Bolton

Mast Cell Tumors

Mast Cell Tumors (MCTs) are not bone tumors. They present themselves most often in the cutaneous tissue of the dog's skin, typically on the body but occasionally on the limbs as well. Those dogs with tumors on the limbs generally have longer survival rates than those that have MCTs on the body. Their presentation is extremely varied; they can feel or look like just about anything. Some appear as hard nodules, others as oozing ulcers, some as soft, fatty lumps. They are typically first noticed by the owner as a raised bump (hairless or not) on the skin of the animal.

MCTs most commonly affect older dogs (nine or more years), though as with all cancers, some very young dogs can and do develop such diseases. There is no predisposition for males or females. Though the disease can occur in any breed, some seem to be more prone to MCTs than others, such as Bullmastiffs, Rottweilers, Boston Terriers, Golden Retrievers, and Boxers. Approximately one in three mast cell tumors is malignant.

Because these tumors may look so different, diagnosis cannot be made on appearance alone. Testing such as a *biopsy* (the excision of tissue from the patient for microscopic examination) and *aspiration* (the withdrawal of cells from a tumor by means of a needle) must be performed to confirm the presence of mast cell cancer as well as provide information on staging the disease. *Staging* refers to the process a veterinarian uses to determine the extent to which the patient has been compromised by the cancer and which options may be most effective in treating the disease. The three major considerations in the staging process are 1) the size and type of the primary tumor, 2) the involvement (or non-involvement) of lymph nodes in close proximity to the primary tumor, and 3) the expected or known risk or evidence of metastatic tumors elsewhere within the patient.

Other clinical testing that may be performed to determine if the cancer has already spread systemically includes blood tests, buffy coat smears (which look specifically for mast cells present in the blood stream), bone marrow aspirations, lymph node aspirations, x-rays and/or ultrasonography (specifically of the heart, lungs, and other internal organs for evidence of metastasis). In cases where tumors are small and solitary, their growth is slow, and there appears to be no systemic spread to other organs or lymph node involvement, then surgery and subsequent adjunctive therapy may be used to treat the patient. Excisional surgery to remove the tumor must be performed with a very wide and deep margin. A *margin* refers to the "edges of the surgical specimen" and is a predetermined amount of healthy tissue that is removed along with the tumor to provide as "clean" an edge as possible. A "dirty" margin describes a surgical excision in which tumor cells have been left behind. Due to the fact that disease at the cellular level is extremely difficult to detect, taking a large margin greatly increases the chance that the majority of cancer cells have been removed. For this reason, amputation provides a unique surgical option to combat mast cell tumors of the extremities. By removing the limb, the largest margin possible has been utilized. Surgical excision, or amputation, is generally followed by a standard course of radiation and/or chemotherapy treatments.

Soft Tissue Cancer

Hemangiopericytoma, also called *spindle cell sarcoma* or *dermatofibrosarcoma*, is a form of skin cancer that commonly affects older dogs. Males and females seem to be equally affected, and there is no definitive breed predisposition. These tumors frequently occur on the limbs. Due to their high recurrence rate (sixty percent) and their low metastatic rate (fifteen to twenty percent), this type of cancer is best treated by amputation whenever possible.

Most of the testing methods to confirm the presence of cancer have already been mentioned above. To review, they include such procedures as a physical exam, blood tests, x-rays, and biopsy. The physical exam sometimes enables the vet to zero in on the location of the tumor by reading the level of pain or discomfort evoked during palpation or manipulation. Blood tests will sometimes show changes in the animal's immune system or organ functions. However, many times blood tests are inconclusive and should not be relied upon as the only diagnostic tool. X-rays can show some tumors, mainly in bone. The problem with using x-ray as a diagnostic tool is that it cannot be used for early detection or prevention. In order to identify a tumor on x-ray, that tumor must already be made up of more than thirty thousand abnormal cells in order for the human eye to detect it. Tumors in soft tissues cannot usually be seen in standard x-rays but can occasionally be detected through the use of ultrasonography. Biopsy and aspiration testing allow for greater interpretation of the type and degree of cancer and help the vet determine the most suitable treatment options for that patient.

Surgery to treat cancer can be performed in several different ways. A surgical biopsy removes only a portion of the tumor for evaluation. *Exploratory surgery* is performed to give the vet a better look at the tumor and allow him or her to make a decision regarding the best surgical approach for the patient. During the course of exploratory surgery, a decision may be made to perform other types of surgery while at the site of the tumor. These may include *debulking*, a partial removal of the cancer when tumors are too large to remove in their entirety or when they are located in areas of the body that prevent them from being removed completely, and standard excisional surgery, which can include such procedures as amputation.

Following surgery, most dogs also undergo a series of adjunctive therapies to control or eliminate systemic spread of cancer cells. These treatments typically include chemotherapy and radiation. *Chemotherapy* is the administration of a toxic substance intended to kill rapidly growing cells such as cancer cells. Unfortunately, it is not a selective type of drug and will also kill healthy, fast-growing cells that are not cancerous, such as bone marrow cells and hair follicle cells in terriers and poodles. The same type of chemo drugs that are used in the treatment of human cancer are used in the treatment of canine cancer, though at lower levels, in fewer combinations, and spread out over shorter periods of time. Complications to chemotherapy include suppression of bone marrow production, which may cause a decrease in white blood cells, causing the dog to become susceptible to infection. Other problems include gastrointestinal damage producing severe bloody diarrhea and dehydration, which requires hospitalization, and lesser symptoms such as lethargy, loss of appetite, nausea, and mild diarrhea. Severe side effects are seldom seen in dogs, as they are in humans; approximately less than five percent of dogs receiving treatment experience them. Chemotherapy treatments may be administered in oral form (pills), as an injection, or as a slow intravenous infusion, which requires hospitalization. The dog is generally awake during all of these administrations.

Ionizing radiation treatment utilizes very high levels of various types of radiation to kill cells and may be either electromagnetic or particulate in nature. *Electromagnetic radiation* includes gamma rays and x-rays. *Particulate radiation* includes beams of electrons, protons, neutrons, and alpha particles. Both normal and cancer cells can be and are killed by radiation, but treatments are designed to limit the damage to healthy tissue and to concentrate on the tumor. Radiation therapy may be utilized prior to surgery to reduce the size of a tumor or to try halting uncontrollable tumor growth, making tumor removal easier. When radiation therapy alone is used to treat tumors—to reduce their size and to decrease pressure, bleeding, and pain—it is known as *palliative treatment*. Radiation is also used following surgery to kill any remaining cells that may still be present following excision and in areas where complete removal of the tumor would jeopardize other vital organs.

Because the dog must remain completely still during radiation treatment, the animal is anesthetized to prevent movement. Anesthesia can cause minor complications such as vomiting and disorientation upon regaining consciousness. Complications from radiation include damage to the dermis (skin) and hair loss. These conditions generally repair themselves when the course of treatment is completed. Therapy is normally spread out over a period of several weeks to help protect normal tissue from large, single doses of radiation.

A long-term complication is that of damage to healthy bone and tissue, which may not be realized for months or even years following the treatment. Such was the case with Ellie, a Beagle who was treated by surgery and radiation to remove a mast cell tumor from her left side. The cancer was successfully removed and Ellie lived a normal, active life until a day, four years later while running across the yard, when she broke her left front leg. Radiation had caused a continual deterioration in the nearby leg bone. Due to the severity of the break and uncertainty about whether it would ever heal properly, the limb was removed, and Ellie now lives a normal life as a canine amputee, still cancer free. This is a unique case in which amputation was performed as a response to a treatment complication and not as a response to the actual disease.

Across the country, many veterinary universities are conducting clinical trials on various cancers and treatment options. A *clinical trial* is a course of treatment offered to pet owners at low or no cost for very specific types of cancer. These trials are usually fully or partially funded by major drug manufacturers or special interest groups in order to develop cures or treatments for various diseases. The treatments are offered at very low cost to pet owners in order to attract participants to their programs. The owners of dogs faced with the prospect of amputation due to cancer complications may find it worth their while to have their regular veterinarian investigate any possible trials being offered in their part of the country.

The sad truth for the majority of dogs diagnosed with cancer is that they will succumb to the disease within one to four years. Many people may find these statistics very disheartening, but a pet owner should remember that, for dogs, the concept of time is much different than it is for humans. We should not be unwilling to do whatever we can for our dogs so that they can experience as much time left as they may have. When faced with decisions regarding medical treatments, prognosis, and expected life spans, the pet owner must remember two very important factors. First, the amount of time we are actually blessed with the company of our beloved pets is an unknown, and we should be grateful for whatever we are given. A myriad of external forces could snatch our dogs from us in a heartbeat. It is very important for us to be mindful that each moment spent with our pets could be our last. Second, when faced with a decision such as amputation that may only extend the life of the dog about a year, we must not be tempted to view this period of time in human concepts. To humans, one year is nothing. Many pet owners figure, why bother? All my dog and I will gain is twelve months together. Well, consider this. The average human, from his birth to his death, lives to be about eighty years old. The average large- or giant-breed dog lives to be about eight years old. In other words, a dog lives its entire life in just one-tenth the time of a normal human lifespan. By agreeing to extend your pet's life by even one year, you have effectively given that animal the same amount of relative time that *you* would receive if you were offered a medical treatment that could extend your life by ten years. This is a concept often overlooked by dog owners and one that should be seriously considered when making any life or death decisions regarding the choice to treat or not to treat.

Another important consideration is that until fairly recently, there was no measurable survival time for an animal diagnosed with cancer. Just a few years ago, the animal would have simply been destroyed for lack of acceptable and effective treatments. Thanks to the advances of medical science, however, and to the driving devotion of pet owners across this country, the canine cancer patient's odds are increasing all the time. Every dog owner who elects to try a new treatment, who participates in a study, or who pushes his or her veterinarian to find or attempt unconventional options, advances our arsenal in the war against cancer. We should not be afraid to say yes to something new. For even if a cure or treatment is not found in time to save the dog we own today, our participation may help in the development of a treatment for the dog we will own tomorrow.

New Animal Cancer Website

Based on the success of their 1994 endeavor, the International Veterinary Brain Tumor Registry has announced the introduction of their newest research site, the VetCancer Registry. This site offers clinicians and researchers access to a wealth of information about cancer trends in companion animals. Anyone with access to the Internet may search this site free of charge. Veterinarians are encouraged to submit case histories that have been diagnosed by histopathology. They are asked to submit cytology, necropsy, or biopsy reports along with the case history. There is no charge for the submission of material. Researchers and interested pet owners may access the information by simply clicking on the website's menu item "View the Data." Searches may be customized by a variety of criteria including species (dog or cat), breed, age, area of the body affected, and treatments used. Each individual animal's case history may be viewed and the attending veterinarian may even be contacted for further information. This site is a simple and useful tool for anyone interested in animal cancer statistics. The website address is: www.vetcancerregistry.com. Complete contact information is in the Directory.

Chapter 5

Conditions and Non-Cancerous Diseases Requiring Amputation

"Molly"   *Photo Jackie Aden*

The number of canine diseases and injuries that might precipitate the need for a life-saving limb amputation far outnumber the different types of cancer that require this drastic treatment. The diseases that will be examined present a mere handful when compared to the almost immeasurable number of events and injuries that could lead to amputation. As you will learn, just about any situation that could cause severe, debilitating injury could result in the need for amputation.

The Unsinkable Molly Brown (Molly to family and friends) whose life was saved by a kind stranger after she was hit by a car. The little stray may have lost a limb in the accident, but she soon found a new and loving home for the rest of her life with the Tolbert family.

Photo courtesy Debby Tolbert

Auto Accidents

The most common injury to cause or require amputation in dogs today is by far an automobile-related accident. In fact, these incidents account for thirty-five percent of all amputations performed. The Humane Society of the United States reports that four hundred thousand animals a day are killed on United States roadways. Of course, not all these animals are dogs, but the figure is staggering nonetheless. *Pet Product News* reported that in 1990 alone, there were 187 human deaths as the result of animal-auto collisions with more than $1.9 billion in associated accident costs.

Most accidents between a dog and an automobile involve the animal being hit or run over by a vehicle. What is especially sad about these accidents is that most are completely avoidable if the dog were not allowed to run loose. Nearly all communities in America enforce some type of "leash law" that prohibits dogs from being allowed to roam at large. These laws protect not only the animal, but the general public as well. However, the above figures clearly indicate a serious lack of responsibility on the part of too many dog owners across this country; they are neglecting to keep their pets out of harm's way.

Many dogs are also injured when they jump or are thrown from a moving vehicle, especially the open beds of pickup trucks. Not only is the dog injured or killed in these situations, but other drivers and even pedestrians can be seriously hurt or killed. Because of the seriousness of this situation, many states have enacted laws that prohibit the transport of dogs in the beds of pickups unless they are securely restrained by the use of approved tie-downs or are transported in appropriately secured crates.

Many dogs are also injured every year when the vehicle they are riding in overturns during an accident. Typically these dogs sustain injuries while being bounced around inside the rolling vehicle, being thrown or ejected from the vehicle, or wandering loose after having been thrown clear of the wreck and hit by another car. The only way to prevent serious injury to dogs riding in vehicles is to always place them in traveling crates. Not only do such crates limit the dog's movement in the event of a rollover but they also ensure that the animal does not get loose and come to more harm.

The remaining injury causes that are not related to cancer or automobile accidents can be roughly grouped into six different categories. It is without doubt that countless other categories could be added to this list and may be as our modern society invents new ways to endanger the lives of humans and animals alike, but for now six separate headings give us more than an informed investigation into causations for a dog to become an amputee.

Birth Defects

A congenital amputee is one that has been born with a noticeable *birth defect* that affects one or more limbs. The cause for the defect began in utero, while the cells of the puppy were still forming and dividing within the bitch's womb. Something went terribly wrong with the cell's interpretation of its instructions, and the result is a puppy born with a missing extremity or a portion of one. Birth defects can also occur that do not result in a congenital amputee at birth, but that require human intervention, thus creating an amputee. Such instances may include a situation where the umbilical cord wrapped so tightly around the limb of a fetus that blood supply was cut off and the limb did not form and grow properly. In these cases, the puppy is born with an atrophied limb, which must be removed.

This type of amputation is very unique because several surgeries may be required to "adjust" the stump as the puppy matures. Because a puppy grows so quickly, the stump that remains following *pediatric amputation* continues to grow as well. This stump may need additional surgeries in order to attain the correct symmetry and to prevent the dog from attempting to use the stump as a false leg. As previously stated in Chapter 3, it is preferable to keep the remaining stump short to prohibit its use in this manner, thereby preventing callusing, wounding, or infection.

Hunting

Hunting today is one of the safest human sports, enjoyed by thousands of enthusiasts across the country. More people are injured each year in other sports such as football, baseball, and hockey than are injured while enjoying hunting. The modern hunter is generally a responsible and careful individual. His equipment is very safe due to years of scientific study and refinement. Most hunters have undergone hours of schooling and certification before being issued a hunting license. The majority of dedicated hunters enjoy hunting because of their deep love of nature and the outdoors. They understand the principles behind wildlife control and conservation, and they take great pride in providing their families with hard-earned and nutritious food each year. As with any sport, industry, or occupation, there will always be individuals who are abusive of their powers and responsibilities, who ignore the rules and laws, and who have no regard for nature or the safety of other humans (hunter and non-hunter) or for themselves. They may poach different species of animal out of the normal hunting seasons, they may take more than the limit allowed by law, and they may participate in unsportsmanlike hunting practices and behaviors—such as road hunting or night hunting. These individuals have no respect for, or understanding of, the natural world and our role in it as predators. Occasionally, dogs and even humans may be injured by such "hunters" as these. It is important to remember that most hunting related accidents are completely avoidable if the *dog is not allowed to roam loose.*

The most common hunting injury for a dog is being accidentally hit with "shot." Shot is a type of round-ball projectile, packed inside a shotgun shell and used primarily when hunting birds, a sport for which numerous breeds of dog have been specifically and successfully bred and developed for many hundreds of years. (The purpose for the development of these hunting breeds was to lend assistance to their human counterparts. Today the majority of hunting breeds are simply house pets, but a minority of hunting and dog-owning enthusiasts do a wonderful job of keeping these breeds true to their original nature and intention.)

Shot comes in different sizes or gauges, depending on the species of bird being hunted. When the shotgun is fired, the shot explodes from the firearm in a "distribution pattern." Some patterns are widely spaced with a ball hitting randomly and at a distance from its neighbor such as for hunting turkey and other large birds. Other types of shot permit a much tighter pattern and generally hit in close vicinity to each other. This smaller shot is used for smaller birds such as snipe and doves. Dogs can be hit by stray shot when they mistakenly enter this pattern field, usually due to inexperience on the part of their hunting companion. These are typically rare occurrences. Of course, they are not the only ones that may cause a dog injury in the field, and not all dogs injured by firearms or other hunting equipment are participants in the sport, as we shall see.

While the velocity or traveling distance of shot is very limited, a bullet fired from a rifle can travel for hundreds of yards, making it an effective long-range weapon. Very few dogs are mistakenly hit by bullets while hunting as there are few states today that allow dogs to be used to "run" large game such as elk, deer, or bear for which rifles are needed. Today, the dogs at greatest risk of being hit by a bullet are those that are allowed by their owners to run loose during hunting season and are mistaken for a deer or some other large prey animal. Accidents can also happen when dogs wander too close to a gun range where shooting skills are practiced.

Of course, there are dogs that are shot intentionally by hunters and other individuals, such as Fish and Game personnel, law enforcement officials, or farmers. These individuals may kill a dog that is "worrying" or running livestock or wildlife or that has become a nuisance or threat to the public's health or safety. Such was the case of Tootsie, a stray mongrel discovered in a small town in southern New Hampshire. She had been living at the dump for months, scavenging on refuse, and was perceived by local officials to be a health hazard. One of the Selectmen took it upon himself to rid the town of the stray. He shot her with a rifle and left her body lying in the dump. Unfortunately, he only managed to seriously wound her but did not succeed in killing her. She was found wandering the streets with a badly damaged front leg. A compassionate couple rushed her to the local veterinarian. The bullet had blown Tootsie's elbow away, and she was suffering from extreme blood loss and

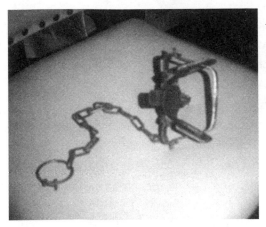

A typical leg-hold trap, above.

Below, "Lucky," the dog who lost her leg due to this trap. Photos courtesy Helen Volz

infection. Emergency surgery was begun in order to save her life. While under anesthesia, the terribly malnourished dog aborted a litter of puppies. A complete disarticulation of the left shoulder was performed, and her life was saved. She was adopted by the veterinarian who performed the surgery, and she has been a loving addition to his family ever since. This illustrates a very brutal manner in which a dog might become an amputee due to complications from a gunshot wound.

Dogs that chase livestock and wildlife pose a serious problem in many rural areas. Dog owners who simply kick the dog outside for the day may not realize that their family pet could be ganging up with other latchkey dogs that spend their days chasing, maiming, and killing deer, sheep, or other dogs and then fall asleep contentedly in front of the woodstove each night. These animals can cause a great deal of damage to local fauna and can pose a serious threat to the livelihood of farmers and ranchers. Nearly all communities possess laws dealing with marauding or vicious canines. They can be shot on sight when caught in the act of attacking other animals or making aggressive overtures toward humans. Furthermore, the owner is held liable for any and all damage inflicted by the dog. It makes good sense to keep your dog on your own property, regardless of whether you live in a quiet suburban neighborhood, a bustling city, or a rural agricultural community.

Another hunting activity that may affect dogs that are allowed to run loose is a run-in with a leg-hold trap. Today, trapping constitutes a very small percentage of the hunting industry in this country. By today's standards, modern traps are considered fairly humane and are intended to hold the animal until the trapper comes to dispatch it. The science and philosophy of trapping have progressed well beyond the enormous, saw-toothed bear traps of pioneer days in all but the most remote and hostile areas of the country, such as Alaska and other northern provinces where man himself is still considered prey by the native wildlife. Many traps have become so "high-tech" that they will not even secure a hoofed animal such as deer or livestock, but will only hold a pawed, fur-bearing animal for which they are intended.

As our rural and wilderness lands have become more heavily invaded and populated by humans, the risk of encountering traps has increased in areas where trapping is still permitted. It is the sole responsibility of the dog owner, and not the trapper, to ensure that the family pet does not become the victim of such a mechanism. A licensed trapper has secured necessary paperwork and paid appropriate fees to the state in order to carry on a profession that supplies him and his family with supplemental income. He has been required to receive permission from landowners to install traps on their land. Your loose dog is a trespasser in these areas, and he will ultimately pay the price for your irresponsibility. Unfortunately, just as there may be unscrupulous hunters, there are on rare occasions, unscrupulous trappers. Should you find an illegal trap on your land or in a publicly owned location (such as a park or playground) carefully attempt to spring the trap so that it poses no threat, and contact your local fish and game department to investigate the incident.

There are no accurate records kept on the number of dogs injured while involved in the sport of hunting. Based on this author's observations, far more dogs are injured by a gun as the result of abuse, than by hunting. There are possibly thousands of people in this country who would not hesitate to harm dogs, simply because they do not like them. There are even people who suffer from mental and emotional diseases who take pleasure in harming animals. These dangerous situations lead us to the next, and probably the saddest, type of injury to dogs that may result in amputation, if not death.

Abuse

Abuse is defined as an act knowingly intended to harm or injure, usually physically. It may also imply negligence or a lack of knowledge, caring, or understanding that may deliberately harm a person or thing. Refusing to seek necessary medical treatments or allowing physical abuse to continue are examples of neglect. In the case of dogs, abuse and negligence usually go hand in hand. It can be very distressing to examine the true nature of the human animal. For all our claims to superiority, morality, and spirituality, we cannot escape the dark side that makes up a part of our being.

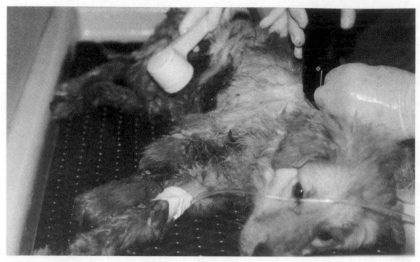

The sad reality of abuse and neglect. In addition to the terrible injuries sustained by Jobie Hobbs—including a limb so badly damaged he required amputation—this poor golden retriever mix weighed only eighteen pounds at ten months of age.

Photo courtesy Christie Burton-Hart

Abuse of an animal can take so many forms and be accomplished in so many ways that it is simply beyond the scope of this book to attempt an in-depth examination of them all. Frankly, it would be too depressing to delve into these atrocities in detail. Suffice it to say, the most common abusive acts that injure dogs tend to be beatings, torture, gunshots, and being thrown from a height or a moving vehicle. One example of such disregard for another living thing is evidenced by the case of Friday, an abused Doberman mix. "Dan" (not his real name), an alcohol and tobacco enforcement agent in the state of Washington, was called in to investigate a problem with a local motorcycle gang in 1986. When he arrived at the location, he found the gang's trailer burned to the ground and the gang long gone. They had left behind a young dog, tied up and sleeping on a dirty old mattress. The puppy was very weak and malnourished, and his left front leg was so badly damaged by birdshot that it required amputation. Friday would have certainly died of exposure and his injuries if "Dan" had not rescued him and adopted him into his family. "Dan" feels that the debt has been repaid a million times over with the love, devotion, loyalty, and protectiveness that the now thirteen-year-old dog has given his family. Friday's story proves that there are caring individuals in our society who will rally against such crimes as animal abuse and will take action to secure the safety of the animal and provide it with medical attention, love, and care. Acts such as these illustrate that man's humanity can shine through.

Animal Attacks

Dogs that require amputation of a limb due to a severe injury inflicted by another animal make up a small but interesting group of amputees. Injuries in this category are generally the result of extreme infection, uncontrollable bleeding, irreparable tissue damage, or untreatable compound fractures. Such injuries can happen accidentally as when a horse kicks an inattentive or intrusive barn dog or when an overanxious bitch mistakenly bites off the foot of her newborn whelp while cleaning it. Injuries can also occur to dogs used to hunt other animals such as raccoons, boar, and mountain lion. While this can be a very dangerous way for a dog to earn a living, it is a skill for which particular breeds have been developed over centuries. Evidence of their original use is found in the breed names that are still with us today—coonhound, wolfhound, beardog, and bulldog. A responsible hunter who employs dogs in his or her hunting excursions, especially for large, dangerous game such as wild boar or big cats, must be knowledgeable about canine first aid and take immediate action to get medical attention for the animal if it is wounded in a skirmish with the prey. Catastrophic infection is of paramount concern in these cases due to the fact that many wild animals are carrion eaters. A mild bite wound can turn gangrenous quickly if not tended to properly.

This puppy was injured by its mother at two days of age and required a limb amputation.

Photo courtesy Susan Godwin

Of course, not all breeds were intended to hunt different species of animal. Many breeds were developed for the sole purpose of fighting each other.

Dog fighting, a public gambling exhibition, originated in the Middle Ages, or perhaps even earlier, and is, unfortunately, still with us today. In America, the practice is outlawed, but there are still underground groups and breeders who continue to support and encourage the sport. Much like the canine racing industry, dogs that are employed in the dog-fighting world are considered commodities. They are "goods" which can be bought, sold, or disposed of with little regard for the animal. It is not unusual for the dog's owner to kill or abandon the animal if it becomes wounded or fails to perform as expected. There are basically two types of dogs implemented by the dog-fighting supporters: the dogs that do the fighting and other dogs used as bait to train the fighting dogs. These bait dogs may be strays, stolen animals, or "free puppies" secured from a local newspaper ad. Their lives are short and very cruel. Rosie, a rescued Doberman, was believed to have been such a dog. She was found wandering the streets of New Bedford, Massachusetts, emaciated, terribly scarred from being used as a bait dog, and hand-icapped with a badly broken and infected rear leg. Rosie was saved by Doberman Rescue Unlimited, Inc., which tended to her medical needs, including her subsequent amputation. A new, loving owner soon adopted her.

Technological Causes

Non-cancerous, non-automobile related injuries are grouped under the heading *technological causes.* This group is intended to comprise limb-threatening injuries that may be the result of a mechanical tool—such as a lawnmower, chainsaw, piece of farming equipment, or boat propeller—or exposure to other man-made objects such as toxic or caustic agents, explosives (including fireworks and land mines), trash, poisons, barbed wire, and non-hunting related gun-shot injuries such as those sustained by police and war dogs. These injuries run the gambit from burns to compound fractures or sever-ing to infection. Except in the cases of dogs actively employed in dangerous professions such as police work, bomb detection, and war dog duties, the majority of these injuries can be easily avoided.

Diseases (Non-Cancerous)

Though the diseases that may result in amputation are not as numerous as those "non-disease" conditions mentioned above, they are every bit as serious and often just as life threatening. For an easy examination, these diseases have been grouped under three easy-to-understand and straightforward headings: infection, degenera-tive bone disease, and cancer look-alikes.

Infection is defined as an attack on the body by harmful microor-ganisms, which successfully invade and establish themselves within the host and multiply or grow. Infections can be classified as acute or chronic. An *acute* infection is of sudden onset and has a short, but very severe, duration. A *chronic* infection exhibits a lingering tendency and may or may not be severe. An *infectious disease* is an unhealthful condition, caused by bacteria, viruses, protozoans, or fungi, which is capable of being transmitted from one individual to another by direct or indirect contact. Such diseases can include distemper, kennel cough, rabies, coccidiosis and Lyme disease—though this is only a small sampling of infectious diseases that can affect dogs.

As far as the owner of a canine amputee is concerned, infection is a far more serious thing than any of the contagious diseases listed above. A dog that has suffered a severe infection such as osteomyelitis (bone infection) or gangrene may require a limb amputation in order to control the spread of the infection. In the case of *osteomyelitis*, a microorganism invades the dog's body at the site of a compound fracture, where bone has been exposed to the external environment, or during a surgical procedure, such as the insertion of a stabilizing pin or plate. Very rarely the infection is caused by blood-borne bacteria. The typical signs of this type of infection include pain, swelling, fever, and lameness. If the particular bacteria or fungi that caused the disease can be isolated, then appropriate antibiotics can be administered. However, in extremely acute or advanced cases, the removal of the devitalized bone, and possibly the limb, may be the only life-saving option.

Gangrene is a serious condition in which body tissue dies as the result of inadequate blood supply. This deficiency can be caused by a blockage of the blood vessels, as seen with an embolism, or by frozen capillaries such as during frostbite, as well as by tight bandaging (tourniquet) or by hormonal disease such as diabetes. According to the American Diabetes Association, from 1997 to 1999, about eighty-two thousand nontraumatic lower-limb amputations were performed each year among people with diabetes. Among humans, this is the most frequent cause of limb amputations. Gangrene can also result from acute infection. If proper blood supply cannot be reestablished to revitalize the damaged tissue, or if the condition is progressive and more healthy tissue is at risk, then the limb may need to be amputated in order to halt the condition and spare the life of the individual.

Peewee, a Maltese, became an amputee when gangrene set in due to the improper application of her cast to heal an injured leg.

Photo courtesy Louise Prior

Degenerative bone disease includes such well known debilitating conditions as hip dysplasia and osteoarthritis. While these conditions are not life threatening, they are often extremely debilitating and painful, resulting in a diminished quality of life for the animal. In situations where all options have been exhausted, the only remaining treatments are beyond the financial or physical capability of the owner, and all other required criteria have been satisfied, amputation may provide palliative relief for these dogs. Removal of the affected limb can alleviate the pain and pressure caused by an eroded and arthritic joint. One of the most important criterion to remember during consideration of such a drastic treatment is the health of the opposite limb. If the opposite limb will be compromised in any adverse way by the removal of the damaged limb, then amputation is not a logical option. Euthanasia may need to be considered at this point to end the suffering of the animal.

Look-alikes, for lack of a better term, are conditions that can *mimic* many of the symptoms of cancer but that are not caused by, or in any way associated with, a truly cancerous condition. These conditions are quite rare and typically will not be encountered by the average dog owner. However, their misdiagnosis could result in the unnecessary amputation of an otherwise healthy limb, so it is important for the dog owner to be aware of them.

The first of these is a *bone cyst*. The definition of a cyst is any abnormal membranous sac, which may contain fluid or semisolid material. In the case of bone cysts, such a sac is located on the long bones of the limbs. The single "sac" can be filled with serosanguineous fluid as in the case of *solitary bone cysts* or large, blood-filled lesions as in the case of *aneurysmal bone cysts*. Generally, such sacs are benign in nature (non-cancerous) and are asymptomatic, giving no outward indication that the animal is suffering from this condition. Bone cysts go undetected until trauma causes the sac to rupture, creating pain and inflammation in the limb, or a fracture occurs due to a weakening of the bone. A hasty examination of such a condition on x-ray, conducted by an inexperienced or inattentive health care provider, could result in a misdiagnosis of the condition. If no further testing is done (such as needle biopsy or aspiration) a quite unnecessary amputation might be performed. The painful and debilitating condition caused by a bone cyst can, in most cases, be treated successfully by drainage, curettage, and bone grafting without sacrificing the entire limb. These treatments stimulate osteogenesis (the production of new bone) at the site of the defect. If your veterinarian has any doubts about the appearance of a tumor-like structure and its nature, a second opinion should be sought, and further investigative testing should be conducted.

Valley Fever. The author first heard about this disease while attending a lecture by Dr. Jean Dodds, a renowned veterinarian from California who many years ago began the only canine blood bank in this country, HemoPet. Former racing Greyhounds are the blood donors for this remarkable program. They are rescued from racing owners who wish to dispose of the dogs. Their health is evaluated, and if they pass all the health exams, they become blood donors for a time. Then, hopefully, they are placed in loving, adoptive homes. According to Dr. Dodds, one such Greyhound intended for the program developed a very pronounced limp and was examined by the kennel veterinarian. X-rays were taken, and he was diagnosed with bone cancer (osteosarcoma), a very common disease in Greyhounds. The staff of HemoPet agonized over what to do with the dog. The only way to extend his life—for perhaps another year or so—was to amputate the leg. But amputees are very hard to place in new adoptive homes, especially a dog whose days are numbered. Clearly, he could not be used in the blood donor program. It seemed the only option was euthanasia. The staff members at HemoPet decided to seek a second opinion, to ensure that they had done all they could for the dog. Based on the new examination and a second series of radiographs, the anomaly on the first x-rays was diagnosed not as a bone tumor but as a condition caused by a disease known as *Valley Fever.* The dog was treated with the appropriate anti-fungal drugs and recovered completely—without amputation.

So what is this insidious disease that can masquerade as cancer? Valley Fever is a potentially lethal, systemic disease caused by the inhalation of a very specific fungal spore found in the dry, desert-like ground conditions of such states as Arizona, New Mexico, and California. Dogs, humans, and other animals can be infected. It is not contagious, in other words, it cannot be passed from one individual to another. The spore must be inhaled directly by the animal from the ground. Symptoms usually occur within three weeks of exposure and include fever, lethargy, weight loss, and seizure. But the most significant, and often misdiagnosed, symptom is an unexplainable lameness. This lameness occurs when the fungal infection begins to attack the bones and joints of the host. On x-rays, this damage can look quite similar to a malignant bone tumor. Only veterinarians very familiar with Valley Fever would know to suspect this illness when presented with questionable radiographs. All dog owners who live in areas of the country affected by this fungus, who travel to such areas, or who show or purchase dogs in or from these states, should be aware of this disease. Though it can be fatal if left untreated, it is also quite manageable and curable if it is caught in time and the appropriate drugs are employed to stop the fungal infection. For more information about Valley Fever contact:

> Valley Fever Center for Excellence
> Mailstop 1-111
> 3601 S. 6th Ave.
> Tuscon, AZ 85723
> Hotline: 520-629-4777
> email: vfever@arl.arizona.edu

As one can see, the conditions that might require an amputation for today's dogs are great and varied. Because of the changes and advances in our human society, the risk of harm to our pets is increasing at an alarming rate. The average dog owner should strive to protect his dog to the best of his ability. In this way, it is hoped that the incidences of cancer, debilitating trauma, and amputations will decrease among America's canine population.

Chapter 6

Canine Pain and
Its Management

"Ruby"   *Photo Paula Gray*

No examination of canine pain and its management would be complete without a look into the emotional lives of animals and how, throughout history, humankind's perception of and belief in these emotions have changed to suit our socioreligious and scientific doctrines of the day.

Once upon a time, ancient man respected and revered the animals that shared his world. His gods took the forms of animals, and his own behaviors and emotions were described in animalistic terms—sly as a fox, brave as a lion, memory like an elephant. These expressions are with us to this day. We may have forgotten why we use such descriptions, but our ancestors knew why. Clearly ancient man identified with the animals around him and often wished to emulate them. By attributing such qualities or behaviors to animals, ancient man believed without question that animals possessed emotions and feelings just as humans did.

However, this belief began to shatter with the introduction of modern, human-centered religions. When man raised himself up upon a pedestal to be more closely aligned with the new gods he had created, animals tumbled from importance in his life. Many of the modern religions professed a new belief that only humans possessed souls. Animals were suddenly considered to be as far beneath mankind spiritually as rocks or a puddle of water. They were no longer appreciated as sentient beings. In addition, they were no longer believed to possess emotions or feelings. Those peoples who still honored their ancient religions and traditions and who maintained their symbiotic relationships with animals and nature were termed "pagans" and "heathens." They were horribly persecuted, and their ancient animistic gods became the devils and demons of the new religions.

This new way of thinking—that animals were emotionless and unfeeling beasts—prevailed throughout the medieval and renaissance periods, right up to the scientific and industrial eras of the modern age. Scientists of the day, the priests of the newest forms of religion, encouraged this belief. It allowed them to dabble in their art without guilt or recourse for the horrible suffering they inflicted upon their helpless victims. Learned scientists of the time professed that the creatures' reactions to the living tortures performed on them, though appearing similar to pain, terror, and despair, were indeed nothing more than the mechanical, automatic responses of an unfeeling beast, no different that the reaction of a tree's leaves brought down by the blowing of the wind. They told their audiences, and no doubt believed themselves, that the ignorant animal felt neither pain nor discomfort. This certainly made the scientist's job much easier to perform.

This convenient and escapist mentality carried well into our own "enlightened" age. Even early veterinarians, the caregivers and life-savers of animals, believed that the creatures entrusted to their care were mindless, emotionless things. Veterinary science arose as a means for man to care for his living property that provided him with a livelihood. If the baker's oven collapsed, he fixed it or risked a loss of income. Likewise, if the farmer's cow collapsed, he also needed to fix the thing or risk financial decline.

Over the last several decades, as pet ownership has increased and animals have assumed a role of friend and companion to us, a modern resurgence regarding just what feelings and emotions animals actually experience has finally begun to surface. It closely shadows those beliefs once held by our very wise, ancient ancestors.

Today, pet owners openly acknowledge and recognize emotional responses in their animals. What dog owner does not agree that the cries and howls of an eight-week-old puppy left alone in his crate are anything but loneliness? Or that the mere whisper, "Want to go for a ride?" produces anything but sheer, exuberant joy in the family canine. Recognizing these emotions in their pets, humans, not surprisingly, also identify pain and discomfort when they see it in their animals.

Modern day animal health care providers must deal specifically with the issue of animal pain and discomfort. Even if some do not believe that animals can have feelings and emotions as complex as humans, they must face the fact that they need to address their *client's* perception of the pet's pain and provide an appropriate response. This tremendous change in attitude is beautifully illustrated in a rather innocuous pain management handout, produced by the Fort Dodge Animal Health Company (a drug manufacturer) and distributed to veterinarians. In one of the pamphlet's opening paragraphs, in bold print, it states, "Any condition capable of causing pain in humans is also able to elicit pain in animals." This simple statement is a far cry from the beliefs of our not-so-distant relatives.

Though animal pain relief of the past generally consisted of a dismissal of the very notion that animals experienced pain, a pet luckier than most may have found some slight relief in the form of a human aspirin given once or twice a day. Today a growing demand for pain relievers specifically designed for and beneficial to animals has forced veterinarians and drug companies to take a closer look at the issue. One would think that the development of such drugs would be a natural, simple step to take since the majority of drugs used to treat humans are routinely and rigorously tested on animals. However, as recently as the 1990s, a United States senator attempted to pass a bill making it unlawful to use human medication to treat animals suffering from the same maladies as their human counterparts. Apparently old habits—and beliefs—die hard.

Luckily, there are more people today who wish to see their beloved pets happy, comfortable, and pain free than there are those who would have it otherwise. Several types of medication have been introduced to address these concerns. The first group consists of **anti-inflammatories** and includes nonsteroidal, anti-inflammatory drugs (**NSAIDs**), which are effective in relieving many different types of mild pain. They provide both an analgesic effect (pain relief) and reduce swelling. They include such items as aspirin, acetaminophen, and carpofen (Rimadyl). All dog owners must be certain that their veterinarian provides them with a thorough description of any possible complications that may result from the use of such drugs. Drugs such as Rimadyl have recently come under attack from consumers and the FDA due to the drug's potentially harmful side effects. For some dogs, this drug provides exceptional relief from arthritic conditions, but for others, it acts like a fast-moving toxin, destroying the liver and causing death. Be certain you understand what you are giving your dog and what it could possibly do to him or her. Drugs should only be used if it is believed that they will benefit the animal. A small amount of education in this matter can go a long way to protecting your pet from harm.

The other class of anti-inflammatories consists of *corticosteroids*. These are synthetic steroids (hormones produced by the adrenal glands) and include such items as prednisolone and dexamethasone. These drugs are used primarily to reduce inflammation and itching, but because they are steroids, they should not be used following surgery (especially bone surgery) because they slow the healing process and produce complications at the suture site. They are most useful when used to treat soft tissue injuries.

The second category of medications, known as *analgesics*, comprises two different types of drugs. The first, *opiates* or *narcotics*, is used to treat severe pain that is not alleviated by simple NSAIDs. These are much stronger and include such drugs as morphine and codeine. The second type of pain killer, *sedatives*, works to sedate the animal, keeping it calm and preventing movement that might complicate or hamper the healing process. This class includes such drugs as acepromazine and diazepam.

Of course many of these medications possess dual properties. For instance, steroids can have analgesic properties, and narcotics can be sedating. It is therefore very important for your pet's veterinarian to make a careful study of the animal's overall condition in order to prescribe the correct medication for that particular animal.

The newest method of pain relief treatment is, quite literally, in a class by itself and often involves a procedure, rather than a drug. Perhaps less well know, but becoming increasingly popular with very health conscious pet owners, holistic and homeopathic treatments sometimes are simply lumped together under the term *Eastern Medicine*. Though different herbs, flower extracts, and infusions may be employed to treat pain, treatments such as Reiki, acupuncture, acupressure, and massage are also being used with increasingly satisfactory results. Pet owners should be sure to inform their regular veterinarian if they are also considering alternative medical treatments for their pet. All parties responsible for the health care of the animal must be informed and willing to work together. One day, human and animal medicine may combine Eastern and Western treatment options. Then we will all enjoy the benefits of both worlds.

Pain and its management are especially important issues to consider in the canine amputee. Amputation surgery involves the severing of not just skin and muscle, but bone and nerves as well, two systems of the body especially sensitive to registering pain. Severe diseases such as cancer can cause agonizing pain in areas of the body not easily accessed by surgery. Therefore, it is extremely important to discuss with your veterinarian the appropriate types and amounts of medications for your pet before, during, and after amputation surgery. Your vet may develop a therapeutic plan for your pet's pain management. Such a plan typically has two parts:

Part one involves anticipating the degree of post-operative pain that the animal may suffer. This assumption will depend upon the type of surgery performed and whether that treatment is expected to produce mild, moderate, or severe pain. The assumed "pain threshold" of the pet must also be considered. As many pet owners are aware, not all animals, even within the same species, exhibit the same level of pain tolerance. A Greyhound may scream bloody murder while simply having its nails trimmed (low pain tolerance), while a Rottweiler or Jack Russell terrier could run full steam into a tree trunk and do nothing more than shake his head and trot off (high pain tolerance).

Owners should learn to recognize signs of pain in their dogs. Izzy's slack ears, avoidance of eye contact, lack of desire to move or interact, obsessive behavior to hold and carry certain toys (in this case a pink porcupine), and preference for a cool surface such as these bricks upon which to rest the limb affected by cancer (right hind) all indicate that she is in a great deal of pain. This photo was taken pre-amputation.

In anticipating your pet's level of pain, your vet may elect to administer a pre-surgical analgesic. The benefits of administering an analgesic prior to surgery are that the pain relieving properties of the drug will already be in effect when the animal awakens and there will not be a "waiting period" for the medication to kick in, during which time the animal could be suffering from severe pain. An added benefit of the pre-surgical drug treatment is that it may actually help the general anesthetic work better, requiring a lighter application of the anesthetic, a valuable plus when cardiopulmonary depression under general anesthesia is a concern.

Part two involves frequent reevaluation of the animal and its degree of pain. Pain itself can actually hinder healing and cause the animal further debilitation. An animal in severe pain could injure itself in an attempt to find relief. It may wear itself down by being unable to rest or relax. Its heart or immune system could be taxed to a dangerous point in attempting to deal with the pain. Therefore, it is very important for the veterinarian and clinical staff to select the appropriate drugs, dosages, and means of administration to keep pain under control. Animals whose pain is properly treated are much more likely to recover quickly. In addition to a narcotic or NSAIDs, your veterinarian may also elect to use a sedative to keep the animal calm. The use of such drugs is evaluated while still at the hospital and reevaluated again for the animal's recovery in a home environment.

When your dog is released from the hospital and allowed to return home, it is very important that you be able to recognize pain and describe it accurately to your vet so that the appropriate treatments may be used. Even an apparent absence of pain may be an indication that your dog is suffering. Remember, in the wild, if an animal were to show signs of pain or weakness, predators would quickly single it out and make it a tasty meal. Your pet may be one of these "pretenders" that hide their pain even when suffering greatly. You must pay close attention to your pet's behavior and learn to read its silent body language. You must also be able to recognize the common, more visible signs of pain in your pet.

They are:

- reduced activity and/or depression
- loss of appetite
- limping, favoring, or obsession with a particular body part
- shallow, rapid, or labored breathing
- restlessness/inability to sleep
- high heart rate
- trembling/shivering/severe change in body temperature
- vocalization: whining, whimpering, or lack of normal sounds
- other changes in behavior or activity including aggression, clinginess, or a desire to be left alone

By working closely with your veterinarian and other health care providers, and by being able to recognize signs of pain or discomfort in animals, you can provide your pet with effective pain relief and thereby promote a speedy recovery, even from such serious surgeries as amputation.

Rosie of Medlar Tree

"I have learned so much from Rosie. She has brought me so much joy and has taught me to enjoy the simple pleasures in life—smiling a lot, finding the best spot in the house to nap, snuggling in bed, eating special treats, and getting lots of kisses."

Lissa Karron

Chapter 7

Post Surgical Complications for the Amputee

"Josie"   Photo Betty Jean Greig

Today, even though amputation is a rather routine procedure for most veterinarians, it is still a complicated and serious type of surgery. When faced with the prospect of having to authorize the removal of a pet's limb, many owners feel suddenly overwhelmed with all their questions and concerns. One of the most frequently asked questions is, "What kind of complications might I expect following the surgery?"

In the best-case scenario, the answer is "none." Many dogs experience no physical complications whatsoever. The majority of canines exhibit no emotional problems either. Several things enable this type of favorable outcome. First, the veterinarian and his or her staff (technicians, anesthesiologists, and kennel help) must be experienced, conscientious, and observant. The greatest care must be taken with the patient from the moment it arrives at the clinic. The type and amount of anesthesia must be carefully considered and administered. The patient must be prepped for surgery with the utmost attention to cleanliness and sterility. Clean clipper blades should be used to shave the entire quarter of the animal surrounding the surgical site. The site must be repeatedly scrubbed with

Amputees quickly relearn how to do everything they did before their surgery—including how to balance properly to relieve themselves..

Photo courtesy Tony George (Megan)

disinfecting solution. Second, the technician responsible for setting up the operating room must take great care to ensure that the room is, and remains, clean and sterile. He or she must make sure that the vet's and the attendant's surgical gowns, all surgical drapes, and all medical equipment have been thoroughly sterilized. Third, the skill of the surgeon will also dictate the success of the surgery. A veterinarian who has never performed an amputation outside of veterinary school may not perform the surgery as neatly and efficiently as a professional who has done a number of such procedures. This can open small avenues for risk. Fourth, the post-operative pain medications and antibiotics must be carefully evaluated and administered to ensure a speedy and problem-free recovery for the amputee.

Owners should also be aware of the very real risk of their dog contracting a nosocomial infection while at a veterinary clinic or large teaching hospital. A *nosocomial infection*, which is acquired at a medical facility, may be detected while staying at the hospital or not until the animal has been released and has returned home. Infections that are not easily spread and that can be eliminated with proper disinfection of the facility include such things as distemper, herpes virus, and the tick-borne illnesses such as Lyme, babesiosis, and ehrlichiosis. However, the infections that should worry pet owners most are those that are easily transmitted by contact, in the air, or through contaminated body fluids and which are highly resistant to disinfection. They include staph, strep, E. coli, rabies, and parvo.

Those pets who have undergone major surgical incisions (such as amputation) and whose health is compromised due to the presence of a disease such as cancer are at the greatest risk of contracting an infection. If the facility is not properly cleaned and disinfected and the appropriate preventive measures (such as the prescribing of antibiotics) are not taken during and following the animal's treatment, this can be a real problem. Some facilities, such as the large, prestigious veterinary universities, may assume that their surroundings are clean and sterile and that there is no need to prescribe antibiotics. Any patient undergoing any type of invasive surgical procedure is at risk constantly of being exposed to infectious organisms, regardless of how sterile an area is *believed* to be. In this author's opinion, prescribing an antibiotic in such cases is good practice. Recently the author learned of two cases in which major surgery was performed on two canines at the same teaching hospital. One was to remove a mast cell tumor, and the other was a limb amputation. In both cases, the owners did not receive antibiotics for their animals, and both dogs subsequently developed catastrophic staph infections, requiring extended hospital stays and hundreds of dollars in unexpected expenses in order to save the dogs' lives. In the author's opinion, these unfortunate incidents may have been avoided had the facility been cleaned and disinfected properly and had the attending surgeons simply prescribed a postoperative antibiotic for each animal.

It is the right and obligation of pet owners to view the surgical and recovery areas where their dogs will be treated and to expect to be given the appropriate medications and follow-up treatments for their animals. Owners must do this before their pet's surgery. If they feel at all uncomfortable about the cleanliness of the facility, or the staff indicates that there is a reluctance to prescribe preventive medications, owners may wish to choose another facility. This simple and inexpensive preventive course of action could save dogs from much unnecessary suffering.

Lastly, it is up to the pet owner to ensure that all follow-up, at-home care is performed as ordered by the veterinarian. A pet owner who is not willing to properly care for the new amputee will experience a greater risk of complications than the conscientious owner who takes good care of the animal and follows the vet's recommendations to the letter.

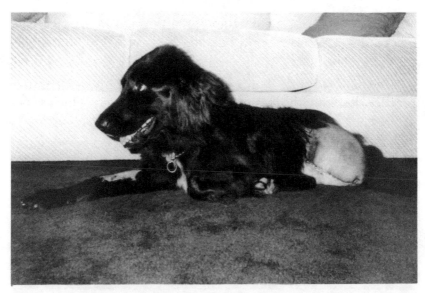

Expect your amputee to have large clipped areas and some bruising immediately following surgery.

Photo courtesy Ann Brandt

Because mild to severe complications can vary considerably from animal to animal, it is important that the owner and health care providers communicate well with each other and that they are able to identify and deal immediately with any problems in a timely and appropriate manner. In this way, further risks and complications can be avoided.

What are considered "complications" for the amputee? An unavoidable result of the surgery itself is the extreme bruising and discoloration that will occur at and surrounding the surgical site. The bruising occurs due to unavoidable trauma to the animal's tissues. When an organ, including skin and muscle, is cut, restrained, cauterized, or placed in a tourniquet, it is mildly damaged. The body's reaction is to rush blood to the injured site, resulting in mild to severe discoloration. This discoloration may create yellow, red, purple, or black bruises, which are now much easier to notice on the animal's skin because all the haircoat in this area has been removed. The bruising begins to fade quickly after a few days, and it presents little hardship to the animal, but it can be traumatic for the dog

Your veterinarian will clip away a large area of hair surrounding the surgical site to ensure that the area remains clean and sanitary. It can take many months for this hair to regrow. Owners of Nordic breeds (husky, Samoyed, elkhound, etc.) should be aware that the coats of these particular breeds can suffer from "follicular arrest," a condition in which the hair growth slows down or ceases altogether. It may take months, or even years, for all the hair to fill in. In rare cases with these breeds, the hair loss may be permanent.

Photo by author

owner to experience when he views his beloved pet for the first time following surgery. Witnessing the absence of the limb and the sutures, bruising, and raw wound edges, can be very unsettling to some individuals. To ensure that their pet does not pick up on these negative feelings, owners must steel themselves against these emotions when going to visit the pet for the first time after surgery or when picking up the animal. These are minor, cosmetic changes only, and the owner should not become preoccupied with them. The dog is not concerned by the way he or she appears. The owner must learn to get over the initial shock as quickly as possible in order to provide the animal with positive feedback and all the love and attention he or she needs and deserves.

Mild complications following surgery can also include such minor effects as clipper burns on the skin, which result from using a dull or dirty clipper blade. Applying a soothing ointment to the area is the easy treatment for such burns. Adverse reactions to the general anesthesia used during the surgery can also present themselves. These situations will be addressed immediately by the veterinarian and the medical staff during and following the surgery. The patient will be reexamined again prior to being released from the clinic. The most common reaction to anesthesia is vomiting; reactions can also include disorientation, aggressiveness, and, in severe cases, cardiac complications and even death. Medical staff members who are thoroughly trained in the administration of anesthetics know how to properly use these drugs to avoid such problems.

As has been mentioned, infection is probably the most common complication following any major surgery. It can range from mild and expected to full-blown, life-threatening episodes. Infections usually present themselves as leaking of fluid from the incision site or a swelling or pocketing of an area beneath the skin. There is almost always an elevation in body temperature. Minor infections can generally be controlled with appropriate antibiotics, which the pet owner can administer at home. More serious infections may require that the animal be hospitalized so that the veterinarian can perform the proper bathing and draining of the affected site and the administration of antibiotics. When the animal is deemed physically stable, he or she may be sent home with drains or wicks that the owner will need to monitor to ensure the infection is being removed. The veterinarian will explain and demonstrate the procedures required to maintain these treatments, and the owner must feel comfortable and confident that he or she can perform the necessary steps on his or her own.

Some swelling and leaking around the incision site can also be normal and unrelated to infection. It is simply the body's way of disbursing excess fluids building up beneath the skin. These swellings are known as seromas. The area should be kept clean and hot, or cold packs may be recommended to help the fluids dissipate. Excessive fluid build-ups may need to be drained by the veterinarian but are not generally a complicated matter.

Serious surgery such as amputation can create varying degrees of pain and discomfort for an animal. As already discussed in "Chapter 6: Canine Pain and Its Management," many pain relievers are available for dogs, and they can and should be utilized when necessary. At home, the owner must closely monitor the dog, be ever vigilant for any of the warning signs that the animal is experiencing pain, and take appropriate action to control it. An animal in constant pain will take longer to heal than an animal that is comfortable and may even cause damage to itself. This can create further complications. It is better to control pain at its onset than to allow the animal to suffer or become injured through self-mutilation.

Many dogs tend to pick or chew at their incision site when they return home. If the animal is allowed to continue doing so, infection can set in, sutures may be torn out, and scarring or injury may occur. Luckily there are several products to prevent obsessive animals from maiming themselves. Bitter tasting salves can be applied to the skin around the incision site to discourage the animal from worrying the area. Stockinette material or bandages can be applied in some situations to prevent self-mutilation. Cones or collars can be placed around the neck of the animal to prevent it from being able to turn and access the area. Most pet owners are probably familiar with those large, funny Elizabethan collars, which look like miniature satellite dishes. Most dogs hate them. They limit the pet's range of vision, and because they are so large and awkward, the dog constantly bumps into walls and furniture, causing him or her to become more stressed. Their housemates may find a friend wearing one of these contraptions to be terrifying and may even attack a dog that is wearing one, certainly not an action beneficial to healing. Thankfully, newer types of restriction collars have been developed. They are simply wide bands of rigid material that go around the neck of the dog and secure firmly with Velcro. They prevent the dog from turning its head but allow for normal vision and eliminate the risk of bumping into anything.

Owners should also be aware that, occasionally, the amputee's housemates may become very fixated on the incision site as well. Dogs that are known to engage in communal grooming sessions should be watched closely to ensure that the helpful housemate is not aggravating the incision site or removing any sutures for his buddy. It may be necessary to keep housemates separated until the wound has completely healed and the veterinarian has removed all the stitches.

Amputees seldom experience any adverse behavioral complications following their surgery, but there are exceptions. Any new behavioral or personality changes that occur in the dog should be brought to the attention of the veterinarian. Some owners report that their dogs seem depressed or lethargic following surgery. This is often a temporary condition in dogs who tire easily in the beginning of their recuperation. Each dog will experience different recovery times. Some bounce back to their old selves very quickly, while others take a little longer and may seem out of sorts for a few weeks or even months. Behavioral conditions that continue or worsen may require medication, behavior modification, an alternative treatment such as acupuncture or massage, or something as simple as a change in routine to jolt them out of a slump. Dogs that exhibit evasive or aggressive behaviors following amputation may be in great pain and should be examined by their veterinarian. Some dogs, especially the toy breeds, may become very clingy after surgery and just want to be loved and cuddled all the time. The owner must decide how much babying the pet receives, but one should realize that such behaviors could become ingrained habits very quickly. You may want to think twice before allowing Twinkie to always have her way when she demands a belly rub or a hot dog. Dogs are not stupid, and many of them train their owners better than the owners train the dogs!

One behavior change that may be noted in the new amputee, which should not be considered a complication, is that most amputees have a tendency to sleep much more than the average dog. This is especially true of the cancer patient. Not only is the dog battling physical fatigue from the increased exertion of maneuvering on three legs, but he or she is also experiencing cellular fatigue as the molecular defense system attempts to battle an insatiable adversary. Allow your dog to sleep and rest as much as it wants. This is the body's way of repairing itself.

Many dog owners do not think about a situation that could create potential problems or complications—the reaction of other dogs in the house to the arrival of the new fledgling amputee. When the amputee arrives home from the hospital, he or she will smell different to his housemates, behave differently, and most certainly move differently. He or she may seem to be an entirely different dog. He may slip and fall a few times as he becomes accustomed to ambulating on what was once familiar flooring. She may "scramble" on linoleum or hard floors if moving too quickly. These types of actions can provoke a wide range of reactions in the other members of the house pack. Some of the amputee's friends may be scared of his or her strange behavior at first and shy away. Most will be exceptionally curious and make it a point to sniff their housemate up and down every time he or she does something out of the ordinary. Housemates who are dominant may not realize at first that the amputee is their old buddy. They should be monitored closely. Some housemates may turn aggressive toward the amputee. The owner must prepare for these situations ahead of time. Remember, dogs are pack animals, and they have a highly driven instinct to subdue any other member of the pack that may be weak or injured and a deterrent to the welfare of the pack. This behavior has even been reported in new mothers who may kill their puppies if they are returned to the whelping box bloody and crying from a recent tail docking. It is simply canine nature. The owner must be ever vigilant to head off problems before they arise. Even before bringing the amputee home, the owner should consider what the reactions of the other dogs in the house might be and take appropriate action to avoid any conflicts until everyone has had time to get reacquainted. For helpful ideas on how to lessen any dog-to-dog conflicts, see "Chapter 8: How to Create a Safe and Accessible Environment for Your Amputee."

Phalco using his canine cart.

Photo Carrie Haggart

A few physical problems could arise for the amputee of which the owner should be aware. These include trauma to the remaining limbs such as pulled muscles, cruciate ligaments torn from over-exertion, and muscle strain on the back and neck. These injuries are brought on by new pressures that the body faces as it attempts to adapt to life as a tri-ped rather than a quadruped. Rest, pain relievers, and anti-inflammatories can alleviate most strains. However, it is far more desirable to avoid such injuries, especially torn or ruptured cruciate ligaments (the main, stabilizing ligament in the knee joint). ACL injuries can occur in large- and giant-breed dogs who have undergone a rear limb amputation. If the dog damages the ligament in his only remaining rear leg, prognosis is not good. This injury requires surgery to repair it, and without another leg to stand on, there is no reasonable method for accomplishing this. The only option might be to support the dog with one of the new canine carts or wheelchairs. In general, amputees do not require such contraptions. In fact, many who are fitted for them never adapt to them but get along just fine on their three good limbs. Carts can be cumbersome and frustrating for the pet using them and frightening for the other animals in the house. They can, however, benefit those amputees who sustain other injuries (to the spine or a remaining limb) and simply have no other means of mobility. These carts seem to be most beneficial to dogs suffering from severe spinal injuries and rear leg paralysis. If you would like more information on canine carts, you may wish to read the children's book, *How Willy Got His Wheels* (Doral Publishing). It is a wonderful, informative, and inspirational tale about a little dog who learns to use a cart because his rear legs are paralyzed.

Canine carts can even be made for front limb amputees, like "Chalwa."
Photo Carrie Haggart

Prosthetics (artificial limbs) seem to receive about the same response from canine amputees as do carts. Most three-legged dogs do not need them, and dogs that are forced to wear them generally do not experience the same type of freedom and enjoyment as do their less encumbered counterparts. Prosthetics can be uncomfortable and awkward for a dog. The harnesses and the cup that the stump fits into can produce sores if not properly padded. Also, the amputee must have a sizeable stump to which the prosthetic can be fitted. Unfortunately, there are no prosthetic companies that design and build artificial limbs specifically for dogs, so locating a crafter can be difficult. You must convince a human company to design one for you. All negatives aside, very large, heavy dogs with a front limb amputation make good candidates for a prosthetic limb as it helps them support the seventy-five percent of the body's mass that would otherwise rest on the one front leg.

It is far better to discourage your amputee from overexerting himself than to have to resort to mechanical means to keep him mobile. Owners should not expect too much from their dogs in the beginning or push them beyond their means. Their expectations must be in line with the animal's abilities and rate of recovery. Physical strength and coordination will improve with time and practice. You must both be willing to take it slow and easy, one step at a time.

There are other complications that the amputee may experience due to adjunctive medical treatments required after surgery or due to the advancement of a disease such as cancer. *Adjunctive treatments*, supportive measures in addition to the main treatment, include chemotherapy and radiation. Some animals may experience adverse reactions to these procedures, typically vomiting or nausea, but their reactions are usually nowhere near as severe as those experienced by most humans undergoing the same procedures. Hair loss, the primary reaction seen among human chemo patients, is generally not an issue for dogs. The extreme burning and skin damage that can occur with radiation treatment is usually temporary; the skin repairs itself when treatments have ended.

Of course, the complications that may arise due to the advancement of a cancerous disease are inevitable. Each new episode of problems must be addressed differently. Concern for the quality of the dog's life—and not the quantity of it—must be considered before proceeding with further treatment options. We have arrived at a point in modern medicine where we can now extend life far beyond our moral duty to do so. The owner of an amputee must consider whether his or her dog would be happier during his final days, living at home in familiar surroundings with his loving family, even though his time may be short, or spending long weeks or even months living at a veterinary clinic, hooked up to wires and machines, no longer in touch with his family or anything familiar, simply to extend the length of his existence. Certainly, this cannot be considered living. Perhaps the greatest complication that your amputee will present to you is deciding when to let him or her go.

"God made dogs with three legs...and a spare."

Dr. Chris Schneider,
Fairwood Animal Hospital,
Spokane, Washington

Chapter 8

Creating a Safe and Accessible Environment For Your Amputee

"Tori"   *Photo Cathy Drdul*

Many owners, when faced with the prospect of living with a canine amputee, express concern regarding how well the animal will be able to get around following his surgery. There is no question that the loss of a limb is a major life change for your dog. Unlike human amputees, though, nearly all dogs adapt very well and very quickly to ambulating on three legs. Even so, there are things that the owner can do to make this transition an easy one for the dog. Many can, and should, be done before the patient is released from the hospital. Most of the suggestions you will find here are easy and inexpensive to implement, and they create only a minor or temporary change in the house.

The first thing that is recommended in adapting your home for the amputee is to provide secure footing on any floor that could be slippery or difficult for the animal to walk upon. This does not mean that you need to recarpet all your hardwood and tile floors. You can very simply eliminate the problem of slips and falls by purchasing several rubber-backed runners or area rugs (such as non-slip bath mats) and placing them in strategic locations where your dog can gain a sure foothold. Non-slip surfaces are particularly important at the base of stairs, in front of doorways, and across long expanses of slippery floors, such as hallways and kitchens. For most amputees, these rugs will only be needed for a short time, just until they become accustomed to traveling on three legs. Most owners are surprised by how quickly their amputee learns to negotiate all sorts of different flooring surfaces within the house.

It is also recommended that you initially limit your amputee's access to stairs until he or she has become adept at maneuvering up and down them. This is especially important whenever the dog will be left alone. You would not want your dog to take a tumble down the stairs with no one home to help him or her. The simplest method for limiting access to stairwells is to purchase or borrow a few expanding baby gates, of which there are many varieties. Some must be permanently fastened to a wall, while others simply hold themselves in place between two walls with a type of spring or tension action.

Many owners find that all they need to do is lean the gate across the opening to the stairs and it provides a sufficient deterrent to their amputee. Most pet supply catalogs carry a few different gates of varying heights and lengths to fit across nearly any opening. You can also purchase basic, standard models in the baby section of most department stores.

Long, steep, uncarpeted staircases should remain off limits even to experienced amputees unless the owner is there to physically assist the animal. These types of stairs are treacherous for three-legged dogs and even for many four-legged ones. A serious fall down a set of stairs can be terrifying, even fatal, for a disabled pet. If the only access in and out of the house or apartment, or to the "preferred" room in the home, is by way of wooden or tile stairs, this is one area where it is strongly recommended that owners expend a little extra time and money to make the stairs safe. A carpeted staircase runner should be installed on interior stairs, and rubber safety treads should be secured to all exterior staircases. Proper flooring and stairway preparations should be attended to before the amputee returns home from the hospital. Creating a non-slip environment for amputees is a priority, at least for a little while. Most dogs adapt after only a short time and no longer need such babying.

Most owners of amputees learn quickly just what extra help— if any—their dogs require. Do not be afraid or embarrassed to provide your pet with the type of care you feel it needs. Take Megan, for example. When their Bedlington terrier became an amputee, her owners, Sheryl and Jim Bolton, did the usual things such as install carpet runners on slippery floors and provide a small set of doggie-stairs so that she could access the couch. At age thirteen, when Megan found taking long walks with the family's other dogs too tiring, the Boltons simply brought her along in a baby stroller!

Other than the flooring alterations mentioned above, there are very few things that need to be done to your home to accommodate living with an amputee. You may find it helpful in the first few days to rearrange several items of furniture to make it easier for your amputee to negotiate through certain rooms, but they learn to snake around things pretty well, and even backing up doesn't present a problem to an experienced three-legger.

Dogs who need to be crated when left alone may find it rather difficult to turn around in their crates as an amputee. Because amputees tend to "hop" rather than "step" when moving slowly, they often require a greater turning radius than their four-legged counterparts. This can make it difficult for them to turn around once inside the crate, especially for medium- and large-breed dogs. This dilemma can be easily remedied by purchasing a new crate one or two sizes larger than the old one, thereby giving the dog the extra turning room that he or she needs. In addition to a larger crate, there are portable exercise pens (known to most dog show exhibitors as x-pens), essentially, small, folding corrals, which have no top or bottom like a traditional crate. Having no roof may make this type of enclosure easier for an amputee to turn around in than a crate. They are especially handy for containing several small- or medium-sized dogs for short periods of time or when traveling. Crates and

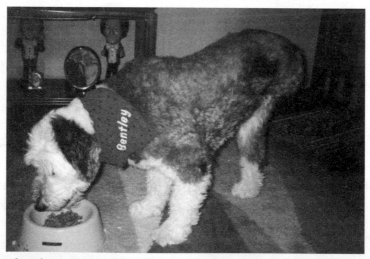

Large-breed amputees may have a hard time balancing and stretching to reach a floor-level food or water bowl. Elevated diners can help.

Photo courtesy Sandra Durante

x-pens can be purchased at pet stores, feed and livestock stores, dog shows, and through pet supply catalogs.

An amputee quickly learns to balance his body by carrying his head and tail in a new manner. You will notice early on that your three-legged dog moves differently than a four-legged one. This is especially noticeable when the dog is standing or moving slowly. The head and tail are used as counterweights when shifting balance and position of the body. Most amputees learn how to compensate for this new balancing act and adapt accordingly. Large breeds may have the hardest time with balance, because they have so much more body mass to manipulate. For this reason, large- and even medium-sized dogs can be thrown off balance if required to drop their heads to the floor in order to reach food or water bowls. In order to compensate for this awkward and uncomfortable position, many amputees simply learn to lie down when eating or drinking. Toy breeds, on the other hand, seldom have a balance problem, because their center of gravity is so much lower to the ground, and they do not have as much body mass to control. For the large breeds, an elevated eating station is recommended. By raising the food bowl, the amputee will not be required to concentrate on his balance so intensely, and it will place less strain on those muscles required to hold him straight and still.

There are many options today in your choice of elevated feeders. Most pet stores and supply catalogs carry several different styles, and the pet owner can find the exact size and style desired. Some of these feeders are very beautiful, more closely resembling furniture than mere dog bowl holders. The dog, of course, won't care what the feeder looks like, so long as he can comfortably reach the kibble within it. The aesthetics of the piece is entirely dependent upon your sensibilities. If your concern is function, rather than fashion, something as simple as a shoebox or an old milk crate may serve equally as well as a fancy, hardwood platform. You may wish to provide a non-slip surface for any flat-top, homemade feeding station so that the food or water bowl is not inadvertently pushed off the

A variety of raised diners are available for amputees. They can range in size from those appropriate for toys to those for giant breeds. They can be made of metal, plastic, or wood. They can even be homemade with items easily found around your house.

edge while the dog eats. The kitchen aisle in your local department or hardware store probably stocks rubberized sheeting used to cushion glass stemware, and this material works very well to hold the bowl in place.

For amputees who are unable to get up on their favorite piece of furniture—your bed, the living room sofa, the kids' beds—there are companies that manufacture small pet ramps or steps specifically designed for this purpose. There are also ramps available to assist large dogs getting in and out of vehicles, something the owner of the mastiff or St. Bernard amputee may find exceptionally helpful. Most amputee owners will find that with a little time and practice such items are not necessary. In a very short time, your three-legged dog will be jumping up and down off the bed or sofa with ease. Until that time, perhaps a new, comfortable dog bed on the floor will suffice.

One item you may find useful when your amputee first returns from the hospital and has not quite learned how to maneuver perfectly on three legs is a harness or sling. These items enable you to help support the dog's body until he has learned how to carry himself in a fast and efficient manner. There are specially designed slings for dogs that have undergone a hind-limb amputation as well as special harnesses with handles designed for front-limb amputees.

Of course, a large beach towel, placed under the dog and behind the elbows or in front of the stifle area can also serve as a makeshift support for your new amputee. You will be pleasantly surprised at how quickly your pet's needs for such supportive measures diminish. Dogs are truly adaptive and courageous animals, never complaining, never regretting their plight in life. If only humans could be so full of grace!

When dog owners become amputee owners and they find themselves doing some minor redecorating within the house to make it easier and safer for their amputee to maneuver, they should remember that some changes may need to be made outside as well. Probably the most important and necessary piece of equipment to keep your amputee safe and healthy is a secure fence around the yard. For many dogs, being allowed to run loose is how they become an amputee in the first place. Not only will a fenced-in yard keep your dog out of mischief, it will also protect him or her from would-be aggressors who might seek this opportunity to attack or fight with your disabled pet. Three-legged dogs can be at a very dangerous disadvantage when called upon to defend themselves against a healthy, fully limbed attacker. Yes, there are many amputees who could valiantly hold their own, but why risk possible injury or trauma to your pet? Installing a fence is such an easy solution to the problem.

Another important consideration, for those who live in regions of the country that receive substantial snowfall, is to maintain an accessible outdoor area for your amputee. Even owners who consistently walk their dogs on city streets may find it almost impossible to do so following a blizzard. It can be downright dangerous to venture onto the streets when plow trucks are out in force doing their jobs. Deep snow and large bankings make it difficult to get out of the way of approaching traffic, especially with a handicapped dog. Maintaining a cleared area close to the house can provide a safe and convenient alternative. Snow poses a special challenge for almost all amputees. The light, fluffy stuff is not too problematic. Most

Creating paths through deep snow ensures that your amputee enjoys the winter months. "Tumbleweed" and friends.

Photo courtesy Michael Bills

amputees, even the little ones, can plow through it easily enough and usually enjoy it immensely. However, a good amount of wet, heavy snow, or, worse yet, a thorough icing, can make it almost impossible for the amputee to get a proper amount of exercise or be able to relieve himself. If you own a small dog, just breaking out the old snow shovel and clearing a small patch of lawn will generally suffice. Those who own medium- to large-size amputees may want to give pets more room to move around. The author learned after only a few months into a typical New England winter that the easiest method for clearing paths and exercise areas in the backyard was with a snowblower. If you want to use a snowblower on *lawn*, be sure to purchase the kind that runs on a track instead of tires, as tires will bog down and get stuck in soft lawns. The author has blown hundreds of miles of amputee paths with a track-driven snowblower and never once sunk down into the lawn following a spring snowstorm.

Of course, any icy areas—especially outside stairs—should be thoroughly sanded to provide sure footing for your amputee. It can be heart wrenching to watch your amputee attempt to maneuver on ice. Guaranteed, the first time you see him or her fall and look up at you with those sad, confused eyes, you will be running to the local highway department or garden center for a load of sand. There are other products on the market today for ice control such as salts, chemical ice melters, and even "pet safe" ice melters, which claim not to burn a pet's paws or be harmful to the pet in any way. The effectiveness of these products varies considerably. Most people find that plain, old, ordinary sand is more than adequate. It is inexpensive, readily available, usually easy to transport (bagged sand is available for those who don't own a pickup truck), and is not harmful to pets, lawns, walkways, or decking.

As mentioned briefly in the last chapter, the new amputee owner must also consider the reaction of other dogs in the household to the returning amputee. Remember, your dog has undergone major surgery. He or she will still be in a great deal of pain when he or she returns home. She may be irritable, tired, and groggy from the anesthetic. The last thing that he needs at this time is for a dominant dog to try asserting itself or for an overexuberant puppy to jump all over him. Even the best of buddies can be confused by the amputee's return. The patient will reek of the hospital, medicine, blood, and disinfectant. As a human, you may not detect these subtle fragrances, but your other dogs certainly will. They could react in ways

Baby vehicles can be modified to accommodate amputees who tire easily on long walks.

Photo Diana Lynn Stout

you never imagined. Your amputee's hopping, unsteady gait could also trigger unexpected behavior toward her. You should be prepared to make accommodations for keeping your amputee separate from the other dogs until they have become accustomed to her new smell and manner of moving. Supervised mingling after a day or so is fine, but do not leave the dogs alone together, unattended, until you are certain there will not be any issues between them.

By creating a safe, comfortable, and easy to negotiate environment for your amputee, you provide him or her with the optimum atmosphere in which he or she can heal and learn new skills. As you have seen, it does not take much time, effort, or money to make any of these basic alterations to your living environment. Most changes are only temporary anyway. The benefits that you and your new amputee will receive from them are definitely worth any minor inconvenience or challenge you encounter.

"Pogo's disability does not slow him down...he runs and jumps. Most people who meet him do not even notice that he is missing a leg. Sometimes I think even Pogo doesn't notice. He teaches a valuable lesson that a disability does not detract from one's capacity to give or receive love."

Laurie and Jim Matheos

Chapter 9

Prevention, Still the Best Medicine

"Ernie"   *Photo Jeanne Spooner*

"An ounce of prevention is worth a pound of cure."

These sage words have been passed down the centuries to us; even today their insightful meaning rings true. It is far more preferable to prevent an unpleasantness than it is to attempt to cure it. This is certainly very true in the attempt to prevent your dog from developing cancer or becoming handicapped or disabled. Of course, there is no magic course of treatment or miracle method of avoidance, but this chapter will offer suggestions about how one can actively strive to avoid situations that could lead to an amputation.

These prevention guidelines are not difficult to follow or understand. They simply require that the dog owner be caring, conscientious, responsible, and observant. Unfortunately, dog owners sometimes fail in these endeavors, which is why problems arise for our pets. As their custodians, we are completely responsible for everything that happens to them. Sadly, some adults choose to ignore this basic fact, and they put their pets as risk due to their irresponsibility.

Preventing basic health problems, including those that may lead to amputation, begins the moment a person decides to purchase a dog. Responsible, prospective puppy buyers should seek out a competent, professional dog breeder from whom to purchase a new puppy. A professional breeder has spent years, possibly decades, devoting herself to the health and welfare of the dogs that she produces. She has studied traits, genetics, conformation, workability, and behavior in her dogs. She knows what diseases are common or rare for her particular breed, and she also knows how to breed her animals responsibly so as to avoid major health or behavior problems. She may even make very little financial return on her substantial investments of time and devotion. Professional breeders raise dogs because of their deep love for the breed and because they understand that there are other dog lovers in the world who will cherish one of their puppies as much as they do. They are seldom motivated by money.

Puppy mills, pet stores, and "backyard breeders," on the other hand, do not possess this knowledge, devotion, or degree of professionalism regarding the dogs they produce. A *puppy mill* is a commercial wholesaler of livestock. It produces large numbers of different breeds or species in order to reap a quick financial return. Though there are certainly exceptions, many of these "factories" house and breed animals in conditions that can only be called neglectful and inhumane. Their intended customers are pet stores, laboratories, and other individuals (wholesalers) who purchase large quantities of puppies for a variety of reasons. Very rarely can an individual buy a puppy directly from such a business. Instead, the average dog buyer finds the end product of such businesses at the local pet store.

A *pet store* is a retail establishment that makes its money by selling food, supplies, and, in some cases, live animals. Though the store owner may have started the business because he or she loved dogs, the successful continuation of the business requires that he or she sell commodities—including puppies. Regulations and guidelines regarding the care, housing, and treatment of livestock in such establishments have become much more regulated and specific. Still, puppies are to be bought and sold. Other than the shipping and invoice number attached to the puppy, the pet store owner may know nothing else about the creature—no health history, no parental behavior history, and no medical concerns for the breed. The store employees, typically young teenagers, may know little or nothing about animals. As sympathetic as you may feel when you see these sad, adorable animals, you put yourself at risk when choosing to buy a puppy from such unknowledgeable sources. By supporting these establishments, you also encourage the puppy mills to flourish and continue their dirty work. After all, *you* are ultimately their intended customer.

Perhaps the worst choice for acquiring a new dog is from a *backyard breeder*. This rather loose term is used to define those unprofessional people whose dogs, by mistake or on purpose, have had a litter of puppies. Those who do it for money may own just one dog—an inferior quality bitch that they breed repeatedly and in rapid succession to the cheapest stud dog they can locate in order to make some quick cash. Others may be so unknowledgeable about canine behavior and anatomy that they are not even aware that the female is in heat, has been bred, or is pregnant until they come home from work and find a room full of crying babies with which to deal. For some people, being blessed with a litter of helpless little puppies is like winning the lottery; they instantly see dollar signs. Unfortunately, the owners may have no knowledge about the breed in general or the genetic health or behavior of the animals. Prospective buyers should avoid backyard breeders, because the lack of planning and knowledge about the dog can lead to the heartbreak of a puppy that is unhealthy.

In order to avoid complications and prevent problems down the road, it would behoove the prospective puppy buyer to study different dog breeds in which he or she is interested and learn as much as possible about these animals and the health concerns they each may possess. Some breeds are hereditarily prone to cancer, thyroid problems, behavior and aggression problems, and bone and joint diseases. The wise buyer will weigh all the odds that may be stacked against, or in favor of, a particular breed before making a final decision. Read books, attend dog shows and events, contact or join your local kennel club, and contact several professional breeders to talk about their dogs. The American Kennel Club can provide names and addresses for local dog clubs as well as provide breeder referrals. To locate a club near you, call the AKC Customer Service Center at (919) 233-9767 and request a copy of their *Geographical List of AKC Show and Obedience Clubs* or their *National Breed Club List*. To find a reputable breeder in your area, call their Breeder Referral Service at 1 (900) 407-PUPS. There is a cost of ninety-nine cents per minute, and the average call takes about three to five minutes.

When you have made your final decision and chosen the breeder from whom to buy your new bundle of joy, you should expect to sign a sales contract that will require you to provide food, shelter, companionship, and health care for the dog for the entire length of its life. You should also be sure to secure a health certificate from the breeder, indicating that the puppy has been examined by a veterinarian and determined to be free of medical problems or parasites at the time of the exam. It will also list all vaccinations the puppy has already received. Many conscientious breeders also provide you with a health guarantee for that puppy that is good for up to one year. Should a health concern arise during that time that has been referenced in the health guarantee, the breeder may elect to take back the puppy and replace it with another one. Do not expect the breeder to make a full financial refund or pay for costly medical care should you choose to keep the original puppy and work through the health problems. By doing so, the dog's medical condition becomes your responsibility, not the breeder's.

One final option for acquiring a dog is to adopt an older animal from a breed rescue organization or to purchase one from an animal shelter. Adopting an older dog from a breed rescue organization is usually a good option for those families who do not wish to deal with all the problems of raising a puppy. These older dogs often have a complete family, health, and behavior history. Based on this information, the rescue organization attempts to place these animals in the most suitable home for them. You will benefit from the knowledge about this dog's background and his or her existing or potential health problems. Experienced rescue personnel can provide information about health concerns for the breed, thereby making the potential adopter aware up front of any complications that may arise and how to avoid or prevent them.

Adopting a pet from an animal shelter is an entirely different experience. Many of the pets at a shelter have been picked up as strays, so there is no known history on the animal. Other animals have been surrendered by their owners, who may not be totally truthful about their reasons for releasing the dog. The number one reason for abandoning or giving up a pet is behavior problems. These usually result from the owner's unwillingness to provide proper and necessary training while the animal is young. The other major reason for pets to be released is a health problem that the owner cannot cope with physically, financially, or emotionally. The shelter will attempt to screen the animal to the best of its ability while it is awaiting a home, and it will attempt to place it in the most appropriate environment to benefit both the new owner and the animal. The need for loving homes for shelter animals is immense, and it is certainly a noble and caring act to take one of these poor creatures into your home, but all adopters should realize that they are entering uncharted waters when adopting such a pet. The phrase "caveat emptor" certainly applies. Wherever you decide to buy a puppy, be sure that you have educated yourself not only about the individual or organization with which you intend to deal, but also about the animal— its working heritage or purpose, housing, health and grooming requirements, and all the nuances unique to that breed.

Another recommendation to try to avoid serious health complications with your dog is to purchase one of the smaller breeds. It is a sad fact that the large and giant breeds of dog suffer the most from various cancers and other diseases and potential injuries that may eventually require an amputation. Though the small and toy breeds may have very specific health concerns that affect them, severe problems resulting in the loss of a limb are rare. If you are serious about avoiding many of these situations, choose a dog that will weigh less than fifty pounds when fully grown.

Of course, just purchasing a small dog from a very good, professional breeder is not the only preventive action that a dog owner can, or should, take to avoid future disabilities and complications. Probably the most important thing a dog owner can do to keep his pet safe and sound is to install some type of secure containment system—a fence, in other words. The number one cause of amputation among dogs is traumatic injury as the result of running loose without supervision. Every day in this country, dogs are hit by automobiles, shot by hunters or irate landowners, injured by other animals, abused or tortured, exposed to deadly diseases, or maimed by a number of accidents and dangerous situations. A securely fenced yard can easily prevent such tragedies. There are fence systems in all price ranges and methods of installation to suit any individual's requirements. The type of fence you decide on depends on several factors: the size, agility level, and degree of determination of your dog to escape containment; the size and topography of the area you wish to enclose; the amount of money you can afford to spend on the system; and your requirements for the aesthetics or physical appearance of the fence.

Probably the very best type of fencing for dogs is a solid wooden fence, sometimes called stockade fencing. Because of the height of the panels (usually six feet), it is virtually impossible for most dogs to jump over. The solidity of the panels ensures that your dog cannot fence fight with other dogs or animals outside the containment area or be easily injured by outsiders intent on doing your pet harm. This type of fence is strong and sturdy and not easily damaged or destroyed by dogs. It can also be very attractive when maintained properly. Drawbacks to wooden fencing include the

Small, non-destructive dogs may do well behind wire fencing.
Photo by author

cost, difficulty of installation and maintenance, and inability to directly contain a digger.

Without the proper equipment and knowledge, wooden fences can be difficult to install, which could require the additional cost of hiring a professional installer. Wooden fences demand some degree of maintenance, especially as the fence ages and the wood begins to rot or is damaged by high winds, snow, or falling tree limbs. Further, unless appropriate measures are taken to install block, concrete, or stone deterrents beneath the fence, this type of system by itself cannot adequately contain a determined digger.

Wire fences can provide safe and effective containment for most dogs. These fences may either be constructed of heavy duty, galvanized, linked mesh (commonly known as cyclone fencing or chain-link fence) or lighter weight, galvanized wire with a square mesh design. This lighter type of wire is most often referred to as stock fencing, horse fence, or chicken wire. The roll of fence must be attached to securely anchored posts and must be stretched tight to provide proper stability and ensure aesthetic appeal. Most homeowners can erect such a fence, making it a simpler and more affordable method than installing a solid wooden fence. However, it does present its share of problems.

Many dogs discover that they can easily climb the wire fence and escape. These Houdinis would do best with some other type of fencing. Small or docile pets do well behind this type of containment system but large, determined dogs often do not. Many dogs can stretch, break, or chew through the wire. Biting the wire, especially the thin stock fence type, can be dangerous, even fatal. Many dogs have latched onto a section of wire, only to have it lodge behind their teeth. In their frantic attempts to free themselves, some dogs have been known to cut through the roofs of their mouths or their bottom jaws. It is not a type of fencing recommended for destructive animals. It also cannot prevent other dogs in the neighborhood from provoking fights with your dog. Serious injuries can occur even through chain link, and the owner must take into consideration not only the behavior and abilities of his own dog, but also those of the dogs in the neighborhood that may be allowed to run loose and could pose problems. As with a solid wooden fence, the same type of extra precautions must be taken to bury deterrents beneath the fence line to discourage diggers from escaping.

A fairly new and innovative approach to dog containment is the electronic fence. This type of system requires that a length of electrical line be buried or laid out around the perimeter of the desired area and connected to a transmitter, powered by electricity.

This transmitter sends out an electrical signal around the entire length of the line, which is picked up by a special receiver collar worn by the dog. If the dog wanders too close to the perimeter, the collar emits an electrical impulse (mild shock). There are several manufacturers offering simple installation kits for the average homeowner. They can be purchased at pet stores and from pet supply

Large, active dogs may need a stronger type of wire, such as is used in this chain-link fence.

catalogs. The best-known retailer of this fence system may be Invisible Fence®. Not only does the company provide professional installation, but it also offers professional training, ensuring that the entire package is implemented correctly.

This type of system works incredibly well with almost all dogs—including the diggers! It requires a brief but repetitive training routine to accustom the dog to the audible and physical deterrents. Most often when these types of fences are reported to have been ineffective, it is due to the owner's failure to properly train the dog to the system. Owners who are uncertain about their training abilities should hire a professional trainer. This added expense will be well worth it. Upkeep for this fencing is simple as there is virtually nothing to maintain as long as no one inadvertently digs up or cuts through the wire, breaking the circuit. It may be the fencing of choice in communities that have very restrictive regulations on the types of fences that can be installed. Of course, there will always be exceptions to the behavior of most dogs, who respect the electrical shock emitted by the collar. Some dogs have such high pain thresholds that they never learn to respect the system and will repeatedly break through the line. For these dogs, electronic containment is a poor choice. They need a more solid, physical barrier to deter them. Perhaps the major setback with this fencing is that it provides no direct protection for your dog from other aggressive dogs, rabid wildlife, or humans who would steal or hurt your dog.

There are variations on all these fencing options, and dog owners should thoroughly investigate all choices to ensure that their dogs remain safe and sound on their own property.

Of course it is a responsible act to prevent your dog from roaming loose, and in most communities across America it is a law. These laws are in place not only to ensure the safety and well being of the animal, but are also intended to safeguard the general human population against actions caused by loose pets. Roaming dogs can create a terrible nuisance if not controlled. They can get into garbage and compost piles, spread disease, attack or harass other pets and live-stock, create traffic accidents, sire unwanted litters, be mistakenly shot by hunters, and even act aggressively toward joggers, bicyclists, and horseback riders. Singapore had such a problem with loose dogs roaming its streets that it is now against the law to even *own* a dog there, and the penalties are very severe. Americans take for granted that it is a privilege, not a right, to own a dog and be respon-sible for it. Unfortunately, the attitude of many American dog owners is that someone else will take care of any problems their dogs create. To determine what dog laws your local community enforces, contact your city or town hall. They may refer you directly to your state's office of bylaws and statutes.

Take, for example, the state of New Hampshire. Most of the state is still fairly rural with deep, thick forests. Yet the state lawmakers, like the majority of those across the country, are aware of the impor-tance of controlling loose or nuisance dogs. This should be a matter of common sense in any community. Yet it is amazing how many dog owners moving into the country from the suburbs and cities assume that along with the deed to their new country home, they have been granted an absolute right to allow their city dog to run free. Their justification for this irresponsibility usually sounds some-thing like this:

> *"Grandpa owned a dog in a town just like this, and he never had to chain him up. Old Trusty never left the farm. I want my dog to enjoy that type of freedom now that we live in the country."*

Unfortunately, this is not Grandfather's time any more. Today, even along country dirt roads, the average modern car travels at approxi-mately thirty to forty miles per hour, more than fast enough to flatten Old Trusty. In Grandfather's time, cars were seldom a nui-sance. The majority of families living in rural areas worked at home. They had no need to commute to work in the city at breakneck speeds. The only car the average farmer might see all day would be the postman's. The old John Deere tractor seldom reached a speed fast enough to present a problem to Old Trusty.

Also, dogs in Grandfather's time lived vastly different lives than they do today. Grandad probably hunted with Old Trusty. Perhaps he depended on the dog to round up the sheep or cows, kill varmints in the barn, or stand guard for the occasional marauding fox or coyote. Old Trusty worked for a living and earned his keep. He was too busy to be out roaming the countryside, being a general nuisance to his owner's neighbors. Today's dogs are pampered pets. They seldom perform any type of labor in exchange for their supper. They are bored and restless animals. When left to their own devices and not restrained, they are likely to find improper activities in which to engage.

Most states now enforce laws pertaining to dogs that are considered a menace, nuisance or are vicious. These laws allow for the seizure and disposition of the animal per a court order if the animal is guilty of barking for sustained periods of time during the night; if it digs, scratches, excretes waste, or causes garbage to be scattered on property other than its owner's; if a female dog in season is permitted to run at large; and if it growls, snaps, or chases a person, bicycle, car, or other wild or domestic animal. States with high populations and densely crowded cities may have far more stringent and numerous laws pertaining to loose dogs than do rural areas. Clearly, it is in the best interest of the dog, its owner, and the general public, not to allow an animal to roam.

In addition to installing a fence to prevent your dog from roaming, there are several other actions you can take that will protect your dog from harm and ensure that it does not become a nuisance to the public. Always walk your dog on a leash with a properly fitted collar. Be sure that the leash is free of any wear or defect. Dogs, even small ones, can be very strong. Many dogs have been injured because their equipment was old or faulty, and they got away from their owner. This is a very simple, effective, and inexpensive method for controlling your animal. Take time to properly train your dog. Training should begin while your dog is still a young puppy. This is when his or her behavior is most malleable. Refer back to the data in Chapter 3 regarding the average age at which most dogs are injured in an automobile accident. You will see it is at this critical period between six months and two years that the adolescent dog needs the greatest amount of control and supervision.

Even if you own an older dog, he or she can be easily trained thanks to the wonderful fact that Mother Nature has designed this animal to learn by repetition. The key to teaching a dog anything is to do it often and to praise lavishly when the animal performs correctly. Negative training (hitting, yelling, and intimidating) seldom works effectively and may create more problems than the ones you are trying to solve. It is highly recommended that all dog owners attend at least one dog obedience class during their lives. Not only will the dog learn proper socializing with other dogs, but a professionally taught obedience class will also teach the owners how to train their dogs and understand their behavior. This is crucial to being a responsible and caring dog owner.

Even the most well behaved dogs, including ones that have earned dozens of obedience titles and awards, can and will react contrary to human wishes and act just like dogs at some point in their lives. Humans are seldom aware of those things that might trigger an instinctive reaction in dogs to run, chase, or flee. Because our vigilance is seldom enough of a deterrent to keep our pets from harm, all owners should carry a leash when working or walking a dog, even if they do not believe they will ever need it. Caution should also be used in areas frequented by hunters and other sports people. Keep your dog on a leash during hunting season. If venturing into the woods or fields, you should both wear blaze orange so that a hunter can distinguish you from a deer or coyote. If a dog learns no other command during its lifetime, it should at least know and respond immediately and without hesitation to the word "Come!" This one word can literally save your dog's life.

Keeping your dog safe from injury or illness involves more than restricting the animal from running loose. Providing proper nutrition, medical care, and freedom from exposure to disease are just as important. To help ward off cancer and other diseases, provide your pet with the best nutrition that your family can reasonably afford. The axiom "You are what you eat" also applies to our pets. If the food we feed them is loaded with by-products, toxins, chemical preservatives, and pesticides, their health will be seriously affected. Over the past few years, many of the ingredients and additives in pet food have come under fire from conscientious consumers. Chemical preservatives such as BHA and ethoxyquin are thought to be cancer-causing agents, and yet they are still routinely used to preserve many pet foods. By-products, the waste of the meat and poultry industries, have long been the staple ingredient of most pet foods. Today, consumers are demanding better quality of their pet foods, hoping such intelligent changes will benefit the health of their animals. At one time, what actually went into a commercially prepared pet food was a mystery. But with the introduction of books such as *Foods Pets Die For* and *The Consumer's Dictionary of Food Additives*, consumers are educating themselves about this issue. More information on providing proper canine diets, especially ones that may help support a recovering amputee, and even assist in the treatment of cancer victims, can be found in "Chapter 11: Health Care and Nutrition for the Amputee."

One of the most proven means of preventing health problems for your pet is to provide proper medical care. According to the American Animal Hospital Association, two out of three dogs will develop a severe illness or experience a serious injury during their lifetime. All dogs should be thoroughly examined by a qualified veterinarian at least once a year, more often for older or at-risk animals. Lumps, bumps, changes in behavior, infections, wounds, limping, signs of pain or discomfort, and any other unusual symptoms should be brought to the immediate attention of your veterinarian. Never allow infections, wounds, or frostbite to go untreated in your pet.

Early detection is still the best means of fighting cancer, protecting against serious disability, and ensuring that your dog lives a long, happy, healthy life.

You should discuss proper vaccination schedules with your veterinarian. If you have always traditionally brought your dog to the vet for yearly shots, you might be surprised to learn what is now being considered "proper" for vaccination protocols. All puppies should be vaccinated to trigger disease resistance in their bodies against common diseases to which they may be exposed. They lose their natural resistance once the antibodies they have received from their mother's milk wear off. Throughout the remainder of their lives, dogs may from time to time need booster shots of certain disease-fighting vaccines to trigger their body's natural defenses. Dogs are typically vaccinated for distemper, parvovirus, and rabies. These are the most serious, and potentially fatal, diseases that affect dogs today. Vaccination is the only sensible precaution against such diseases. Today dogs are also routinely vaccinated against other less deadly diseases such as coronavirus, Lyme disease, bordetella (kennel cough), and giardia. The effectiveness of vaccines against these diseases is questionable, but they are usually given along with the vaccines for distemper and parvo in what are commonly called five or seven-way shots. These single injections may include up to seven different disease pathogens designed to trigger immunity within the dog. But subjecting a pet to such a mixture is like giving it a powerful toxic cocktail.

As cited by the *Wall Street Journal* in an article in March 2000 on the possible harmful effects of the drug Rimadyl, the pet drug business is a booming industry, raking in more than $3 billion annually. The industry provides incredible financial profits not only to the companies that manufacture the drugs, but also to some independent veterinarians who push the drugs, making their clients believe that their pets cannot live without them. Luckily, the average consumer is becoming more educated about such things today, forcing such vets to reevaluate their traditional sales methods. Many vets are now advocating that pets receive their inoculations on a modified vaccine schedule—only a few of the vaccines on one day and the rest a few weeks later—and that the animal receive only the types of vaccines that it truly needs to ward off a serious threat of disease. This modified approach allows the dog's immune system to deal with the invading disease pathogens much more effectively, instead of being completely overwhelmed. Unlike in days gone by when many dog owners unwittingly allowed their pets to be routinely injected with toxic combinations of vaccines *every single year*, owners are now becoming aware that this practice can be dangerous, even life threatening, for their dogs. Can you imagine the reaction of most parents if they were informed by the medical community that their child must receive between five to seven shots every single year from the time they are a few months old until the day they die? Americans would be in an uproar over such a preposterous vaccine practice! No responsible parent would ever allow his or her child to be subjected to so many vaccines every year. Yet this is exactly the type of vaccine procedure that some pet owners allowed for the entire length of their pet's life. If we trust that the vaccines we give our precious children are effective for several years—sometimes even for life—then why do we question the efficacy of the vaccines we give our pets? Is it really medically necessary to subject our pets to such yearly barrages of potentially dangerous pathogens? Perhaps not.

This practice has now come under intense scrutiny within the veterinary medical community. At the First International Veterinary Conference on Vaccines and Diagnostics held in Madison, Wisconsin, in July 1997, the following recommendations were made regarding the administration of vaccines:

> *"Puppies and kittens should be vaccinated against infectious diseases such as distemper, parvo, panleukopenia, and rabies not before six weeks of age, but accordingly thereafter, and two to four doses of vaccine should be administered two to four weeks apart. An annual booster should be administered at one*

year of age. Thereafter, give boosters only every three years
unless required more often by law. Geriatric animals generally
do not need boosters. Serum antibody titers can be monitored
instead between boosters or in older animals."

Furthermore, the health care professionals at this same conference
stated that, regarding vaccine titers:

"Vaccine titers for distemper, parvo, and panleukopenia show
adequate immunologic memory. Titers should be rechecked
annually. If titers indicate less than optimal levels for these dis-
eases, recommend booster vaccinations unless the animal has a
history of adverse vaccine reaction, immune-mediated disease,
or some other immune dysfunction."

A "titer" is a blood test that reveals whether or not a specific vaccine
is still active within the dog's system and therefore capable of trig-
gering an immune system response should the dog become exposed
to the disease. Blood titers can be conducted for parvo, distemper,
rabies, and, in the case of cats, panleukopenia. Pet owners now have
the option of having their dogs first tested for their degree of immunity before simply injecting more, perhaps unnecessary, vaccines.
For those owners extremely concerned with the health of their pets,
this choice is a welcome change. At a cost of between twenty to forty
dollars for a titer check, however, the majority of pet owners may
simply opt for the easy and cheap option of the nine-dollar all-in-
one, do-it-once-a-year shot. Of course, dog owners should not
decide on their own when and how often to have their dogs vaccinated. They must engage their veterinarian in a serious discussion
on this subject and let their pet care provider know they are concerned about over-vaccinating their pet. Then both parties can
agree on a safe, effective, and less toxic protocol for treating the dog.

A dog owner should also strive to provide a chemical and toxin free
environment for the animal to live in due to the risk these chemicals
pose. As already discussed in the chapter on cancer, many items that
we use everyday, whether alone or in combination with other

chemicals, are known to be cancer-causing agents. Not only is it healthier for the dog to avoid exposing him or her to such toxins, but it is also healthier for pet owners. Remember, a dog lives its entire life in about one tenth the length of our own. All the cumulative effects that poisons and chemicals have on our dogs during this short time may eventually have the same effects on us at a later date. Sadly, our pets are often early indicators of the consequences we should expect to encounter. Lawn fertilizers, bug sprays and pesticides, antifreeze, flea dips, chemical cleaners, and deodorizers are all known to have had lethal effects on animals and people. Yet we continue to use gallons of these items every day and in dangerous combinations. The average American thinks nothing of having his or her beautiful lawn chemically treated, the rugs chemically cleaned, and the house fumigated for insects all on the same day. Can you imagine the effect all these potentially toxic substances have on a creature that is in direct and close contact with these areas?

One final area of prevention for pet owners is to always monitor the interaction between animals and children. Many needless and senseless tragedies occur because family pets were left in the care of young children. Untold numbers of loose dogs that were hit by cars escaped containment because of the inattentiveness or lack of knowledge on the part of a child. Many puppies, kittens, and some older animals die of drowning every year because a child put the animal in the family pool or bathtub or left the animal unattended in the vicinity of a body of water. Not all dogs know instinctively how to swim!

Other child-inflicted injuries frequently seen by health care providers include elastic bands or other constricting items placed around legs, tails, and necks of family pets, causing strangulation, infection, or tissue growth around the foreign material, and marbles or other small items forced into the ear canals, causing hearing damage, behavior changes (including aggression due to severe pain and frustration), and self-mutilation.

Children do not usually understand the results of their actions. What may seem like play to them can be hazardous, even deadly, to the family pet. This applies to children of any age, toddlers to teens. Preteens and teenagers can sometimes be especially brutal to family pets as they attempt to work through the many frustrations of adolescence. Do not ignore any unexplainable, sudden injuries to the pet if dealing with violent or irrational teenagers. If you suspect animal abuse, you may need to seek professional help for the child, as this is an early indicator of future social problems. Remove the pet from the home in cases of severe abuse.

It is preferable to simply teach all children from a very young age that animals must be respected and treated well. Instill in them a sense of love and nurturing for the animals in the home. Teach them how to properly care for the animal. Never, ever leave a pet in the care of a child of any age. As the adult, YOU are solely responsible for the well being of the children and the pets in the home. Do not expect a child to do your job for you. Children simply do not possess the knowledge, common sense, or understanding that an adult does in regard to the care and treatment of other living things. Hopefully, you will have planted in them the seed of kindness toward animals so that they, as adults, will be able to pass this important lesson along to their own children.

These guidelines for preventing disease and injury to your dog are simple to follow, easy to understand, and require little financial expenditure. What they do require is an investment of time and attention—something we should be more than willing to give to our dogs for all the love and devotion that they bestow on us.

Common Canine Amputee Nick-Names

Three
Lucky
Stump / Stumpy
Tripod
Hopalong
Hopalong Cassidy
Gimp / Gimpy

Chapter 10

So, What Can You Do With a Three-Legged Dog?

"Ivy"   *Photo Donna Logdson*

When faced with the prospects of owning a canine amputee, many dog owners will humanize the complications or effects that the amputation will have on the quality of the dog's life. They worry that, as an amputee, the animal may not be able to do all the things it loves to do. Will it be able to run and jump and swim, chase the kids, go for walks, work the herds on the farm, or continue its competitive career? As far as most canine amputees are concerned, this is unnecessary worrying on their human's part. It is something that only humans, in our complicated social and economic world, would actually consider. We must remember that dogs are not humans. Though they may exist on the same planet that we do, they live in a vastly different world. They are not affected by the emotional baggage that we carry. A dog's quality of life, his ability to function as Nature intended, and his desire to perform the work and activities that he loves and for which he may have been born and bred, will be almost completely unaffected by his amputation. (Of course, for those dogs suffering from cancer, the disease will eventually seriously impact the dog's abilities, even though the amputation itself seldom does.)

Perhaps the greatest thing that dog owners can do is allow our dogs to continue performing those chores and activities that they so love, so long as they are able. There is nothing sadder than witnessing the amputation of the *spirit* of a dog who is not allowed to run and bark

Working dogs still have a desire to work—even as amputees. "Jem"
Photo Peggy Miller

and simply act like a dog. It benefits no one to restrain an animal (especially a disabled one) to such an extent that his or her quality of life is lessened. Let them be dogs!!

Many breeds have been developed over the centuries to work as herders and drovers, hunters and guardians. They have been genetically imprinted to possess very specific behaviors and abilities. These are not traits that suddenly disappear just because the dog loses a limb. These are ingrained qualities that the animal should be allowed to express. If your beloved pet has always performed herding tasks on your farm, or in competition, do not presume for an instant that this is a chore of which he or she is no longer capable. Operating on three legs is seldom a deterrent to a working farm dog. The sheep, geese, cattle, and horses are just as respectful of a three-legged dog as they are of a four-legged one. In fact, the animals being herded are probably not even aware of any difference in the dog at all. The eyes and body posture of the dog are what encourage the herd to move, not how many paws he or she is using. To deny this activity to your herding dog will do him or her far more harm psychologically than the disease or injury has done physically.

Not only must a competent farm dog be able to herd, but he must also be able to sniff out and defend against intruders. Amputees everywhere can do just that.
"Maya"   *Photo Gunhild Ward*

A story about Maya, a Labrador retriever, illustrates this belief perfectly. At the time of this story, Maya was about eight or nine and had been an amputee for many years. As her owner, Gunhild Ward explains:

> *"I had about seventy goats here at the farm as part of a rescue operation. Because my fencing was not built to contain goats, they, of course, escaped constantly. One day they ranged about a quarter of a mile away, onto a neighbor's property. I did everything I could to get them back, but without success. Suddenly, Maya and another young dog escaped their dog enclosure at my farm and came to my aid. Now, to the best of my knowledge, neither of these dogs had ever seen goats, let alone herded them. Yet they somehow managed—on their own—to herd all seventy goats into one group and proceeded to drive them through the woods, across a ravine, through the fences, and into a shed, where they held them until I managed to close them in. I don't know how she knew I needed help. And I certainly don't understand how she knew what to do. She is a wonderful dog!"* Amazing! A Lab who can herd—and an amputee to boot. Never underestimate the capabilities of a disabled dog.

Many dogs and their owners who have enjoyed various types of competitive events, such as obedi ence, agility, and hunting tests, soon discover that being a canine amputee does not prevent them from continuing their pursuit of such activities. Most organizations that sponsor these events welcome amputees to participate in all their various forms of competition, the only exception being conformation classes. The purpose of the conformation class is to judge

Alexx, a Briard, negotiating a dog walk during an agility competition prior to his amputation.

Dakota Sioux, shown with one of her competitive awards, is certified as a Canine Good Citizen and is working toward her C.D. (an obedience title). Photo Donna Mills

the dog's physical type and features against the breed standard to determine their merit as a breeding animal, thereby ensuring the continuation of quality animals within the breed. Obviously, an amputee should never be considered for use in a breeding program. Their disqualification from such a purpose is not only due to the disease that precipitated their amputation, which could be a genetic problem they might pass on to subsequent generations, but also because of the incredible and unnecessary stress that a pregnancy would impose on a physically challenged animal.

(**Special Note:** It is highly recommended that all amputees be spayed or neutered. In fact, it is recommended that all pet dogs be altered while still young. Not only does this procedure prevent unwanted litters and behavioral problems, it can also help prevent deadly diseases such as testicular and mammary cancer. Also, attempting to perform spay or neuter surgery on a dog *after* it has become a hind-limb amputee can be very difficult due to the fact that all four limbs need to be securely restrained during the surgical procedure. Not being able to restrain both rear legs can make the surgery more difficult and time consuming, something that creates unnecessary risk to the animal. Better to simply have the animal sterilized while young and healthy than to worry about complications later on.)

Canine amputees are not limited to the United States. Here, Megan, an amputee in England, sports her Award for Bravery, presented to her at a walk to raise money and awareness for Staffordshire bull terriers in that country.

Photo Tony George

Organizations that welcome canine amputee participants include the United Kennel Club, which allows amputees to compete in its agility, obedience, and hunting events (for hunting breeds only) as long as they are not considered lame by the judge. As stated by Michelle O'Malley Morgan, manager of Multi-Breed Field Operations for UKC, *"If the dogs can move about to do the required work without any additional problems, they are welcome to participate."* Each individual case is left to the judge's decision regarding the animal's performance and ability. The Federation of International Canines (FIC) also welcomes amputees in its performance events. They do not place any restrictions on canine amputees. Their philosophy is that if the dog (same as a person) can do the job, he or she should never be disallowed. Their titles are based on the workability of the dog, not on appearances. The Mixed Breed Dog Club of America lets amputees compete and earn titles and will even adjust jump heights in obedience competitions to accommodate disabled dogs.

Sadly, the largest and most popular dog club in the world, the American Kennel Club (AKC), does not approve of canine amputees competing in its events. While almost all other dog clubs in the world claim that their purpose first and foremost is to honor and promote the *working ability* of the canine race, the AKC continues to claim that its sole purpose is to maintain the stud books for the dogs it registers. However, the AKC hosts more performance events than any other dog organization. As far as the author knows, since AKC declined to comment on the issue, the only AKC recognition that an amputee may earn at this time is the Canine Good Citizen award. The CGC title is awarded to any dog, mix or purebred, which can successfully pass a series of examinations designed to test the dog's reaction to a variety of scenarios. The program was implemented as a public relations tool to appeal to the general, non-showing, pet owner. Most CGC tests are conducted by local, AKC-affiliated dog clubs, which may hold them in conjunction with a dog show or match or may even offer them following completion of a club-sponsored obedience class. To find a local AKC dog club in your area, visit www.akc.org and click on "Clubs" or "Canine Good Citizen Tests."

Since canine amputees are basically no different than their four-legged counterparts, it should come as no surprise that some amputees even become movie stars. The movies *Thunderheart* (Tri-Star Productions) and *The Whole Shebang* (Whole Shebang Productions) both featured canine amputee actors, proving that amputees are just as smart and trainable as any dog. These brilliant furry actors do not shun the local arts either.

Mocha doesn't let the fact that she only has three legs interfere with her ball playing.

Photo Otty Merrill

Katie Squibbs of Ohio reports that her amputee toy poodle, Chester, landed the role of Chowsy in the hometown production of *Gypsy Rose*. Katie says:

> *"He would get up on stage and really strut his stuff. The crowd loved him, and after the play each night he would be in the reception area...signing autographs for his fans."*

Of course, working and competing are not all that amputees enjoy doing. Most disabled dogs continue to pursue all the old activities that they did prior to their surgeries such as hiking, beach combing, boating, swimming, playing fetch, and frolicking with friends.

It may be impossible to curb your amputee's desire to swim, as Clarence proves. Owners can help ensure their dog's safety by providing equipment such as this life vest.
Photo Mary Kenney

As many people are discovering, the canine amputee also makes a wonderful therapy dog. Therapy dogs receive special training and certification, enabling them to visit hospitals and nursing homes where their presence often does more to improve a patient's mental health than years of medication and conventional therapy. The canine cancer amputee is an especially beneficial therapy worker in pediatric cancer wards. Children can, understandably, have a difficult time dealing with many of the challenging aspects of their diseases, which can include amputations. Visiting with a happy, three-legged canine that is jumping around, licking them, and nosing around for treats may give them a more positive outlook on life and may also help to relieve many of the pressures that extended hospital stays can produce. Adults with psychological disorders and the elderly suffering from dementia and Alzheimer's disease also respond very positively to dogs. Therapy dogs are proving themselves to be invaluable members of the staff in facilities that care for such individuals.

Rusty, a Golden Retriever who lost his leg in a car accident, is a pet-assisted therapy dog who visits with children, adults, and elderly patients at local hospitals. He is a wonderful therapist.

Photo Pam Dickens

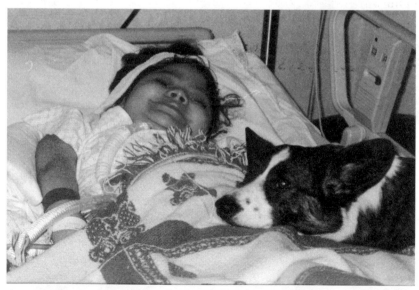

Amputee therapy dogs come in all shapes and sizes, as Josie, a Corgi, demonstrates.
Photo Betty Jean Greig

"Rusty" and friends   *Photo Pam Dickens*

By and large, the most preferred activity of any canine amputee is being a friend and companion. Their preferred location is by their owner's side. Like any normal, non-disabled dog, amputees crave the love and attention of their owners. Enjoy your amputee; spoil him often; love him deeply; and involve him in your daily activities, or better yet, find new things that you can both enjoy together!

Chapter 11

Health Care and Nutrition for the Canine Amputee

"Nikki"   *Photo Bill and Carol Decker*

A discussion on health care and proper nutrition for the canine amputee must take into consideration that there are two unique types of amputee—those who are cancer patients and those who are not. This chapter will aim primarily at proper care of cancer patient amputees because their needs and requirements are much more demanding than those of an otherwise healthy, non-diseased amputee. However, all suggestions and recommendations can also be applied to the non-cancer amputee, thereby improving his quality of life as well.

Medical Care

One of the most important aspects of your amputee's care is to closely monitor his health. The owner should be on the lookout for improvements as well as setbacks or complications. At home, check--ups and physical exams should be performed daily. This is a very wonderful activity in which to engage, and your dog will love it. Choose a quiet time of the day when you and your dog can spend a few moments together. Allow your dog to assume whatever position seems comfortable—standing up, lying down, or sitting in your lap—whatever. Beginning at the tip of the nose and working your way back toward the tail, massage and stroke the dog's entire body—don't forget the legs and feet. Your actions should be firm but caressing, not too hard and not light enough to tickle. Allow your fingertips to feel for any new or unusual lumps, pimples, painful areas, swellings, or heat. Pay careful attention to those areas around the lymph nodes (located under the chin at the beginning of the throat, in the armpits of the front legs, and on the inside of the rear calves). Be sure to make a note of any changes. Anything you notice out of the ordinary should be brought to the attention of your veterinarian, who may also want to perform a physical exam. Even following amputation, early detection and prevention of other health problems is of paramount importance.

It is recommended that a professional health care provider examine all dogs at least once a year. The vet may notice or recognize something that the owner does not. Cancer patients, geriatric animals, and others whose health is compromised may need to be examined more frequently, perhaps monthly or quarterly.

A very important aspect of your pet's health care is its vaccine schedule. As discussed in Chapter 9 on prevention, it is highly advisable to modify your amputee's vaccine protocol to fit with the new recommendations. If your amputee is a cancer patient, you may want to reconsider giving *any* vaccines to the animal. A pet affected by cancer is already in a life and death battle. His or her immune system is struggling against a voracious adversary, and his or her defenses may already be weakened or diminishing. Injecting a sick dog with a vaccine will only weaken the defenses further. Don't forget, the active substance in a vaccination is actually a weakened form of the disease from which you are attempting to protect the dog. Some dogs, especially those in a less-than-optimal state of health, may develop severe reactions to vaccinations or even the disease itself. It makes no sense to inject a cancer patient with a deadly pathogen that he or she may not be able to assimilate in his or her weakened condition. Consider, what are the chances that your dog is going to be exposed to, and *succumb* to, an infectious disease before the cancer takes him or her? Very slim, indeed.

However, if your dog is not affected by cancer, and, other than missing a limb, is in excellent health, a modified vaccine and titer regimen is still recommended. For those who are holistically minded, it is further recommended that if your pet must be given vaccinations, you should follow up these shots with a dose of the homeopathic remedy, Thuja, to help counteract any ill effects of the vaccination. Annual shots may still be required for dogs that attend shows and performance events, for dogs who reside where certain vaccines are required by law (such as rabies), or for animals working as therapy dogs in hospitals and other public settings.

Dental Care

An area of health care easily overlooked by the average owner is dental hygiene. This is an especially important health concern for our pets today. Wild dogs and their cousins seldom experience profound dental disease and decay, as do domestic dogs, due chiefly to their more natural diets. Chewing on the tough hide, sinew, and bones of their prey ensures that the teeth of these wild canines stay clean and healthy. Domestic dogs are fed diets of cooked and processed grains and cereals, in addition to table scraps and fat- and sugar-laden treats and goodies that contribute to plaque and tartar build up. Advanced dental disease can cause not only tumors and abscesses in the mouth, but also more serious conditions, such as liver damage, as the infection spreads from the mouth, through the bloodstream, and into the vital organs. This is a serious, life-threatening condition. There are steps the owner can take to ensure proper canine oral health.

First, schedule regular dental exams and cleanings for your pet as needed. Serious scalings and extractions must be performed by a veterinarian and under general anesthesia. Be sure to discuss such treatments with your vet if your dog is suffering from cancer, as any procedures involving surgery or anesthetizing can have serious effects on the overall health of your afflicted pet. Many professional groomers now offer dental services called "surface cleanings" along with their regular services. No anesthesia is needed for this procedure. It does not provide the same degree of cleaning that a medical scaling does, but it provides good general maintenance on a regular basis. Second, give your dog only healthy treats that will not contribute to plaque build up, such as carrots, good-quality, hard-baked dog biscuits, and natural, marrow-filled beef bones from your butcher's meat case. Third, if you do not have your groomer clean your dog's teeth every month, be sure to take advantage of the many products on the market today especially designed to help you maintain your pet's dental health at home. These include everything from nylon dental bones to special rope toys to toothpaste and brushes designed just for pets.

For more information on maintaining proper canine dental health contact:

American Veterinary Dental Society
530 Church St. Suite 700
Nashville, TN 37219
(800) 332-AVDS

Grooming

Basic grooming is also a very important issue in your pet's overall health care routine. It begins with the most basic of your dog's body parts—the skin. The skin is the largest organ of the body. It is the front line of defense against disease and infection, so it is very important to keep it healthy and fit. The skin is kept in a proper state of health through appropriate diet and hygiene.

It is not only important for the skin and haircoat to be clean and free of parasites, but it must also be properly conditioned. Skin should have a certain degree of elasticity. With too much moisture, there will be a build up of body oils, creating clogged pores and conditions such as acute moist dermatitis. If the skin becomes too dry, dandruff and itching can occur, as well as significant hair loss due to the skin pore's inability to "hold on" to the hair follicle.

A proper diet does a great deal for ensuring healthy skin. The correct canine diet should include adequate amounts of nutritious food; supplementation (when necessary) with vitamins and minerals; and plenty of fresh, chemical free water. Water is especially important in maintaining proper skin and haircoat conditioning. It lubricates the body and hydrates the skin.

Proper hygiene begins with regular and consistent combing and brushing. These activities not only remove tangles and mats, which, left unchecked, can lead to skin irritation and infection, but the

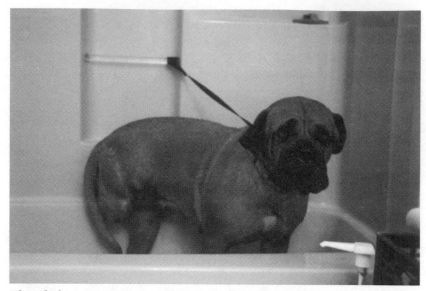

Though she may not appear to be enjoying herself, proper grooming and bathing helps keep Izzy healthy.

repetitive motion of brushing stimulates the release of natural body oils that condition the skin. These oils protect the skin from dehydration, infection, and pollution, ensuring proper wound healing, and coat the fur, strengthen the hair follicles, and make them weather resistant, as Nature intended.

Bathing your dog does more than simply remove dirt and odors and make your pet smell good. It ensures that the hair can perform as it was designed to, insulating your pet against the cold in the winter and heat in the summer. A coat that is weighted down with dirt and oil cannot trap air as it should to create this insulating barrier. This is why it is important to ensure that not only indoor dogs, but outdoor dogs especially, be kept very clean. They need this natural insulating mechanism that only a clean, healthy haircoat can provide.

Bathing should involve two steps—shampooing *and* conditioning. Unfortunately, many pet owners who perform the shampooing part are unaware of the importance of applying a conditioner. Shampoos are intended to remove dirt, grime, and excess oils from the skin and coat. Many can remove too much of the skin's essential oil, stripping it of its protective properties. Today there are hundreds of shampoo options available. There are all natural shampoos (highly recommended for cancer victims), medicated shampoos for problem skin conditions, special color-enhancing shampoos for a variety of coat colors, special texture shampoos especially for wire hair/ rough coat breeds such as terriers, and, of course, flea and tick shampoos. (Pet owners should be aware that *no* shampoo kills ticks—they must be removed by hand. *All* shampoos kill fleas. Plain old soap and water is all one needs to kill and wash away fleas; the trick to keeping your dog flea-free is to prevent future infestations; this will be discussed later on.)

Once the dog has been completely shampooed and rinsed, a good quality conditioner must be applied to the entire animal. The conditioner counteracts any irritating effects of the shampoo, seals and protects the skin against dehydration, and coats the fur to keep it healthy and strong. Without a conditioner, the skin could become dry, raw, and irritated, opening an avenue for infection and disease. Also, without a conditioner, the skin may not be supple enough to properly retain hair follicles, and the result can be profuse shedding.

Owners who have their dogs professionally groomed should discuss their amputee's condition with their groomer and be certain that that individual understands the special needs of an amputee and is willing to provide for them. Amputees tire easily, and since dogs are expected to stand for long periods on the grooming table and in the tub, your groomer must have a great deal of patience and allow the pet to have rest periods during long grooming appointments. A groomer's business is based on volume—the more dogs groomed per day, the more profit that is made. Some groomers may not be willing to accommodate a disabled pet due to the time demands, but most groomers love dogs. They value their repeat customers. Most of them will be happy to cater to the special needs of your amputee, but it is something you should discuss with your groomer as a courtesy. There is one time saving benefit with an amputee—at least four or five fewer toenails to clip!

Do not forget that hind-limb amputees will greatly appreciate a periodic rubbing in those places they can no longer scratch themselves—such as ears, necks, shoulders, and sides. Here Izzy gets a belly rub.

Whether you groom your own dog or have a professional do it, if you own a dog with a long coat or a breed that requires a clipped haircut, you may find, at least just following surgery, that you and your amputee may benefit from a fairly short trim, especially around the hindquarters and the penis. Fledgling amputees may take some time to figure out the most comfortable and least messy manner of relieving themselves. Until that time arrives, keeping the hair short around the "exit areas" can ensure hygienic conditions. If grooming your own dog, *never* attempt to cut hair around sensitive areas with a pair of scissors. The risk of injury should the animal move suddenly is too great. Instead use a pair of electric clippers and preferably a #10 blade. The teeth on a #10 blade are close together, helping to ensure that folds of skin will not get caught and cut. Better yet, send the dog to a professional groomer and simply request that the private areas be clipped and that any long hair on the legs or belly be neatened up as well.

Exercise

Another important aspect of proper health care for your amputee is sufficient and appropriate exercise. All activities and exercise routines must take into consideration your pet's limitations (if any) from his or her disability, as well as subsequent complications from any disease. Remember not to overdue or push your amputee beyond his or her limits. Let your dog set the range for his or her physical exertions. Swimming is an excellent exercise for many amputees as the buoyancy of the water takes the weight off of the legs. You can ensure your pet's safety by fitting him or her with a specially designed life vest. Short walks and hikes, playing fetch, games of hide-n-seek, and learning new tricks or commands are all wonderful activities for the amputee. In addition, make it a point to ensure that your pet receives plenty of fresh air and lots of sunshine—in the winter as well as the summer months. Like humans, dogs can become depressed and lethargic if forced to live indoors in artificially heated and lighted environments. It is certainly no fun to be trapped in the same boring, monotonous routine, with little hope of something new or exciting. This is true for dogs as well as humans.

Environmental

Carefully monitor your pet's environment to ensure that he or she is not being exposed to toxic chemicals and pollutants such as household cleaners, contaminated water, cigarette smoke, and pesticides. You should strive to avoid all chemicals on, in, and around your dog. Items such as spray cleaners, lawn fertilizer, and antifreeze, things that we consider very mundane items in our regular lives, can pose serious health threats for, or even cause death to, our animals. Try to avoid using cleaners, polishers, and air fresheners around your dog. Use only mild, natural shampoos on your pet and mild laundry soap on your pet's bedding. Look for safer, citrus-based cleaners, which can replace irritating and harmful products. Never allow a combination of toxins to overload your dog's system.

You should question your use of poisonous flea and tick treatments as well. Does your dog really need them? Does he or she have fleas or ticks? Or are you simply being influenced by promotion by the drug companies that produce such products. If you do need to use insecticides on your dog, keep the following things in mind: If your dog has just received a vaccination or undergone some other medical or surgical treatment, do not treat him with any type of toxic flea or tick product. Doing so can create serious immune-related complications due to the dog's already weakened state of health. Wait at least two weeks before applying any type of topical or oral insecticide. Be sure to fully investigate and understand what you are considering applying to your pet to keep him or her pest free. Many items that dog owners have used for the past few decades are now known to be either ineffective or dangerous. Beware of such things. They can include flea collars, dips, and sprays. Regarding flea collars, the best word of advice is, don't bother. These items were originally intended to work on the mistaken belief that they can create a "cloud" of protection around the animal to repel pests. Unfortunately, this would only work if the animal never moved. Once the dog shifts position, walks, runs, or moves in any way, this cloud is broken and ineffective. To counteract this failure on the part of their product, many manufacturers have now created collars containing so many toxins that owners are receiving skin burns and rashes from handling them. Some dogs experience overdoses and toxic reactions to the items that are in direct and constant contact with their skin.

Dips are perhaps the most dangerous chemicals manufactured for use on family pets. Today most professional groomers will not even perform dip services that were once a standard within the industry because they know firsthand how deadly they can be. The warning labels on the packages of these items clearly state "HAZARDOUS TO HUMANS AND DOMESTIC ANIMALS." They further state that the products are harmful if absorbed through the skin and may cause eye irritation. The user is advised to avoid contact of these products with the skin, eyes, or *clothing*. All applications must be performed in a very well ventilated area and the person applying the dip is advised to wear safety goggles and/or a face shield, rubber gloves, and appropriate clothing to protect the skin. Dip product labels warn not to use the chemical on puppies, cats or kittens, sick or disabled animals, pregnant or nursing bitches, or animals being treated with a variety of other drugs. Is this really the type of product to which you want to subject your pet? Most flea and tick sprays carry the same ominous warnings as the dips.

Of course, there are alternatives to these products. As already mentioned in the section on proper grooming, a bath with plain old soap and water will rid a dog of flea infestations. Keeping that pet flea free is the real challenge. For those dog owners who live in tropical climates—the condition that fleas especially love—protecting their pets can be an all-out war at times. The most effective way to control these nasty pests is not to use traditional pesticides but to use instead a combination of adulticides and insect growth regulators. *Adulticides* contain an insect neurotoxin that disrupts the adult flea's nervous system and causes death. These somewhat oily products are typically applied beneath the hair on the dog's shoulders; from there they disperse across the entire surface of the dog's skin. Because these products do not penetrate the dog's skin and become absorbed into the body, they are considered very safe. *Insect growth regulators* (IGRs) specifically target various aspects of the flea's life stage. They include products such as CSIs (chitin synthesis inhibitors), which prohibit the production of chitin, a chemical needed by the flea during its molting process, and JHAs (juvenile hormone analogues), which prevent the young flea from reaching adulthood, when it does its damage. Insect growth regulators can be applied to the dog's environment (carpets, beds, and outdoor exercise areas), as well as incorporated into topical and oral treatments. The best defense is a combination of adulticide and IGR. Products that contain adulticides and/or IGRs include Bio-Spot® by Farnam Co., Advantage® by Bayer Co., Frontline® by Merial, and Program® and Sentinel® tablets by Novartis. Some of these items are available directly to the consumer at pet supply stores or from supply catalogs. Others must be obtained from your veterinarian.

There is also a whole range of natural or alternative treatments available in the fight against external parasites, including *Neem* and limonene additives to shampoos, which provide repellent and insecticidal properties. Many people believe that garlic and Brewer's yeast added to your pet's food can help repel pests. The premise is that it makes the pet's skin unpalatable to the flea. Borate powders applied to carpets and outdoor environments are believed to disrupt the early stages of a flea's life by acting as an irritant. Of course, there is nothing as simple to use as a flea comb, which, if employed daily, can easily and economically remove fleas from your pet's coat. Perhaps the most important thing to remember when dealing with a flea infestation is that both the dog and its entire environment must be treated. This means that the pet's bedding must be washed and the house should be "flea-bombed" to kill all existing adult fleas. Where most dog owners go wrong is in assuming that this one treatment will kill all fleas, forever. Not so. Bombs have no effect on unhatched eggs. Even after you have killed all the adult fleas, approximately three weeks after you bomb, the new eggs will hatch. It is advisable to perform a second bombing at three weeks, and again three weeks after that. This should ensure that all hatched fleas have been killed. If you need even more information on controlling fleas, contact your local groomer or veterinarian. They can provide you with the products you need and information on how to use them properly. Because these products can be dangerous if used incorrectly, give serious consideration to what you are about to use on and around your dog. Some of them are good and effective, while others can be quite harmful.

Perhaps one of the most important things you can do as a dog owner to provide your pet with a safe and healthy environment is to keep him or her in a non–smoking home!! The danger of second-hand smoke is well documented within the human medical community. The same risk factors apply to your dogs as well if they are exposed to cigarette smoke on a daily basis. Do yourself, and your pets, a favor, and keep your home smoke free.

All of the recommendations above can help ensure that your pet lives a long, healthy life and can help protect a health-compromised animal from further complications. Remember, as stated in "Chapter 4: The Cancer Patient as Amputee," the risk of developing a cancer- related disease multiplies exponentially when an organism is exposed to two or more cancer-causing agents. For more information about protecting your pets from overly poisonous environments, check out *Are You Poisoning Your Pets? A Guidebook on How Our Lifestyles Affect the Health of our Pets* (Safe Goods) by Nina Anderson and Howard Peiper. This small, easy-to-read book will be an eye-opener for many pet owners.

Nutrition

When it comes to nutrition for the canine amputee, there are several lines of thinking. First of all, if the amputee is not affected by cancer, then a traditional, good quality food should provide an adequate diet throughout the dog's life. Just remember that, as with all amputees, it is very important not to allow your dog to become over-weight. Keep your amputee light. Heavy or obese dogs can have a multitude of health problems including heart, liver, and kidney disease. Overweight amputees will have a difficult and exhausting time trying to negotiate their increased bulk on three legs, thereby seriously threatening the health of their remaining limbs.

Second, if the amputee is a cancer victim and her condition is considered terminal, then by all means spoil her rotten! Allow her to eat anything she wants. It makes no sense to impose diet restrictions on an animal that will shortly succumb to her disease or to attempt to force her to eat something that she will not like. You may as well make your pet's remaining time as enjoyable as possible. For many cancer patients, eating is the last pleasurable act left for them. To put it in human terms, if *you* were dying of cancer and the only thing you could still enjoy was food, wouldn't you want to eat whatever suited your fancy? Of course you would! So give her whatever she loves—hot dogs, ice cream, spaghetti, prime rib, fried eggs. What does it matter? Since the definition of "terminal" means that the animal has less than one year to live, it will make very little difference to her overall condition if you allow her to eat her favorite foods. So go ahead, indulge!

Of course, it is not remiss for a loving owner to hope against all odds that his or her pet will be the exception to all predictions and that the animal will experience an unexplainable and complete remission of his or her illness. Miracles like this can and do occur, even for those patients considered terminal or beyond help. If you believe that there still may be hope for your pet and that diet can influence the time remaining, then use the following recommendations to the best of your ability.

For the cancer patient that is considered non-terminal or is viewed as having a higher survival rate than expected, provide the very best diet that you can afford. Many researchers have discovered that diet has a profound impact on the state of health of cancer patients and that sometimes diet alone can achieve amazing results. In her article "The Canine Cancer Patient" (*AKC Gazette*, May 1998), Dr. Kathleen Hefner states,

> *"Using a nutritional approach for canine cancer patients can be instrumental in their recovery from surgery, in helping them metabolize chemotherapy drugs, and in overall success of the cancer treatment. Good nutrition can also improve a dog's quality and length of life."*

The most highly recommended diet for canine amputees and cancer victims is a holistic or all-natural one. A holistic diet is close to the way nature intended. It consists of whole foods such as fruits, vegetables, raw meats, eggs, whole grains, and live foods such as yogurt. In the past, dogs were fed a diet based on these natural components. Until fairly recently, most humans lived a largely agricultural existence, raising their own crops and livestock and hunting. In our grandparents' time, "dog food" consisted of the leftovers from the family's food preservation and preparation practices—milk, cream, eggs, vegetables, fish and meat waste, blood, and other butchering remains. It has only been within the last forty years that commercially produced, chemically treated, and preserved pet foods have become a commonplace item for most pet owners. After World War II, as mechanization and fast food became a way of life for most Americans, it also affected the way in which we fed our animals. Today's dog food can contain the worst of the remains from the human food industry such as diseased and damaged meat items; by-products, which can include beaks, feet, hooves, feathers, hides, manure, and even the blood-soaked shavings from the slaughterhouse floor (commonly termed "fillers"); hormones and steroids from treated beef and poultry; pesticides from tainted, moldy grains not fit for human consumption; as well as a list of questionable chemical preservatives such as BHA and ethoxyquin.

Today, pet owners need to seriously rethink their feeding practices. They should strive to return to a more natural program, incorporating fresh foods into the pet's diet as often as possible. Some pet owners now opt to feed raw meat diets, home-cooked diets, or commercially prepared, holistic kibble and wet food. This latter type is probably the easiest method for those of us raised in an age of modern conveniences. The author has found that the best type of diet for her own pets (amputee, healthy, and cancer-patient alike) is a combination of commercially prepared, all natural-dog food, fresh vegetables and fruits, and other healthful additives such as pasta, eggs, and venison.

All-natural dry dog foods are now available at many pet food stores, human health food stores, and even online pet supply sites. One of this author's favorite online sites is PetFoodDirect.com. Just a few of the many all-natural pet foods include Halo, PetGuard, Neura, Solid Gold, Innova, and Wysong. You can find phone numbers and addresses for these companies in the Directory section of this book.

The manufacturers will be able to provide you with the retailer in your area.

Like the author, many individuals who hunt provide their dogs with very healthful wild game in place of traditionally raised meat products. Even non-hunters may now be able to find once-exotic game meats at health food stores and by special order with local live-stock producers. American bison and whitetail deer are being raised by an increasing number of farmers and ranchers who were wise enough to pay attention to the market demands for such healthful beef alternatives. Even if you do not hunt, game meats may not be as difficult to locate as you might first expect. One of the advantages of feeding wild meat, in addition to the lower fat percentage, is that wild animals, and even those now raised commercially, are usually hormone, steroid, pesticide, and antibiotic free. This is possible at this time because, unlike cattle, swine, and poultry, game animals have not been interbred and genetically manipulated for centuries, which makes animals biologically weak and health compromised. This may be a meat source that the seriously health conscious dog owner may wish to examine further. To find game producers or even organically raised beef in your area, try contacting your local Cooperative Extension Office, farming and ranching organizations, or local health food stores.

Additional supplementation with extra amounts of appropriate vitamins and minerals may also be beneficial for your amputee and/or cancer patient. In the magazine article mentioned above, Dr. Kathleen Hefner recommends "...diets high in fish oils that contain large amounts of omega-three fatty acids." Not only is it believed that fatty acids help to promote weight gain, often a problem with cancer patients suffering from *cachexia* (a wasting away of the body), but they may help to reduce the size of tumors as well. Dr. Hefner also states that "...in addition to omega-three fatty acids, using other vitamin and mineral supplements may have beneficial effects, particularly ones that contain the antioxidants beta-carotene and vitamins A, K, E, and C, as well as magnesium."

Dog owners are cautioned, though, that anything taken in excess, even natural products and vitamins, can be harmful. Seek appropriate medical and nutritional help before starting your dog on any supplementation regimen. The author recommends that the reader seek out the services of a licensed holistic veterinarian or nutritional therapist for further information. Most conventional veterinarians receive little, if any, training in medical school about nutrition and vitamin support as a medical treatment option. Do not be surprised if your own vet is reluctant or unwilling to discuss vitamin therapy. He or she may simply not know anything about this course of care. This is no reason to deny your pet a treatment that may beneficial. Seek out those professionals who can help you. For a listing of holistic veterinarians in your area, contact the American Holistic Veterinary Association referenced in the Directory at the end of this book.

For pets suffering from cancer, there are some special diet recommendations to be considered. The first one is to avoid sugars and foods containing sugars. Many types of cancer tumors feed off glucose. These tumors convert the glucose into a form of lactic acid that the body has a very hard time metabolizing. Precious energy is used by the body to convert these lactic acids back into glucose so that they can be dealt with properly. A vicious cycle begins. The body expends and wastes energy that it cannot afford to, and the tumor grows larger and stronger by using the glucose as it chooses. To avoid such wasting conditions, it is recommended that diets high in simple carbohydrates be avoided. Substitute diets high in fats and additional fiber. Fiber in the diet tends to decrease the absorption of sugar. Diets high in omega three fatty acids (such as in fish oils) may help control the growth of tumors and enable the body to gain weight or maintain proper weight.

A new diet developed by Dr. Gregory Ogilvie, funded by Morris Animal Foundation, and produced by Hill's Pet Nutrition Inc. is currently available for implementation in the fight against cancer. It is designed to starve cancer tumors of the nutrients upon which they depend, while at the same time, providing the patient with other ingredients such as protein, specific fats, and fiber to help the body defend itself against the onslaught of cancer and maintain a higher degree of health. To learn more about the Hill's Prescription Diet for cancer, contact your veterinarian or Hill's Pet Nutrition Inc. at P.O. Box 148, Topeka, Kansas 66601, Attn: Consumer Affairs. They can also be reached by calling 1 (800) 445-5777 or on the web at www.hillspet.com.

Health care and nutrition play a very important role in the day-to-day care of your dog after he or she has undergone amputation. Nutrition has even been shown to have positive effects on the health of cancer patients. There are perhaps no more important preventive measures to implement to ensure the good health of your pet than proper nutrition and appropriate medical care. Provide the very best care that you can, and when in doubt, spoil them rotten.

Chapter 12

Modern Veterinary Science:

Amputation Alternatives, New Cancer Treatments, Alternative Medicine

"Chris"   *Photo Corinne Killam*

Today, *limb-sparing surgery* is *the* cutting edge technique in the fight against canine bone cancer, especially osteosarcoma. It is encouraging and exciting to hear of a brand new treatment option for cancer, considering the high mortality rate associated with this type of disease, and that there may even be an alternative to amputation. A limb-sparing technique is one that attempts to remove or debulk as much of the tumor as possible, while saving the limb itself. The intention is to provide a pain-free, functioning limb. In many instances, the compromised bone or joint and its tumor may be removed and replaced with a "donor" bone obtained from the canine bone bank or with an endoprosthesis, an artificial bone or joint part, usually made of special metals. Internal, slow release chemotherapeutic agents are often surgically implanted at the site of the graft. This is done with a dissolving "sponge" soaked in a

Dogs such as Brody, whose amputation was the result of a broken bone that did not heal properly and then rebroke, might possibly benefit from limb sparing or bone replacement surgeries.

Photo Eileen Brown

chemotherapeutic agent such as cistplatin, which works specifically at the site of the tumor instead of coursing through the entire body like traditional chemotherapeutic applications.

As reported by medical firms engaged in this new line of research, the front legs seem to respond the best to this promising new surgical procedure. In fact, having a compromised front limb is an important criterion point used in selecting individuals for this treatment. This is critical since the front limbs must carry about seventy-five percent of the dog's body weight, making this a very important treatment option for large- and giant-breed dogs. Other criteria that must be met in order for a dog to be considered a good candidate for a limb-sparing procedure include being in good health with strong renal, heart, and bone marrow functions, no apparent metastatic tumors of the internal organs, no extensive tumor invasion of soft tissue surrounding the bone, and less than a fifty percent involvement of the bone at the site of the tumor. Complications resulting from this type of procedure can include infection, bone graft rejection, and fracture of the newly transplanted bone. Survival rates for limb-sparing surgery done in conjunction with chemotherapy are about the same as those for amputation with chemotherapy. The survival rate of limb sparing with chemo is about twice as long as that of amputation surgery alone.

The medical facility leading the way in this exciting treatment option is the University of Colorado. As of 1998, surgeons there had performed more than three hundred limb-sparing surgeries. Another veterinary hospital active in this line of experimental care is the University of Pennsylvania. Even though survival rates for limb-sparing patients are currently about the same as those for amputee patients undergoing chemotherapy, the invaluable information gained by such research will continue to improve the care that canine cancer victims receive in the future. Perhaps one day, science may even find cures or alternative treatments for cancer that do not involve amputation. Wouldn't that be a wonderful achievement!

Cancer Prevention

Prevention is the preferred method of treating cancer, rather than attempting to rid the body of it once it has become established. Toward this end, a very diverse and growing group of chemical and biological agents are being discovered every day to use in the fight against cancer. They can be collectively called *preventive agents* and include such things as the antioxidant vitamins A, C, and E; plant phenolics such as green tea; omega-three fatty acids; shark cartilage; the herbal supplement Pau D'Arco; soybeans, legumes, and dark green leafy vegetables; aspirin; and holistic treatments that stimulate the body's natural immune systems such as Reiki, acupuncture, acupressure, and massage.

New and advanced forms of early detection with imaging technologies can also help in the fight to control cancer from an early onset. Ultrasound, magnetic resonance imaging, and positron emission tomography can provide early glimpses of first stage cancer development, possibly allowing patients and their doctors to make decisions about treatment options before the cancer has reached an uncontrollable stage.

New Advances in the Genetic Fight Against Cancer

Gene therapy is a cancer treatment option that has only recently moved from the laboratory testing stage into actual clinical trials. It involves techniques that genetically alter a patient's tumor cells by introducing a virus into the tumor, making it susceptible to cancer-fighting drugs. Another method of gene therapy is to transfer genes that increase the patient's immune responses into the tumor or into the bone marrow in order to increase the body's resistance to certain chemotherapeutic agents so that higher doses can be administered. It will still be some time before any meaningful benefits from such treatments can be confirmed with certainty. In the meantime, owners of canine cancer patients may be able to locate special studies and trials in which to enroll their dogs to take advantage of these new and promising treatments.

Vaccine therapy is perhaps one of the most promising of the new cancer treatment options. The process is based on the premise that the body's natural immune system should react to an invasion by a foreign substance (known as an antigen) by producing white blood cells with antibodies to fight the invaders. The problem with cancer—and the reason the body may not react to destroy cancer cells—is that cancer cells are derived from the body's own natural cells, so the immune system may not recognize them as potential threats. Vaccine therapy searches for ways to introduce a mixture of the cancer cells and some other type of agent that the body will definitely recognize as an enemy, such as bacteria. Because the immune system knows that the bacteria is foreign and must be destroyed, it learns that the cells associated with it are also a threat and need to be destroyed as well. The body then produces special white cells, known as T-cells, to deal with and kill the invaders, including all those original cancer cells that the body has now learned are foreigners.

In order to grow and spread, cancer tumors must create extensions of themselves. They do this by converting oxygen and nutrients into growth factors, which can form blood vessels. This process is known as angiogenesis. *Angiogenesis inhibitors* are drugs that are designed to block the formation of these new blood vessels. If new blood vessels can be prevented from forming, the tumor cannot grow beyond the size of a pea, thereby causing no threat to the patient's overall state of health. New drugs are being investigated every year for this purpose and may show promise in providing tumor suppression.

A technology that may have seemed like science fiction only a few years ago is now being actively used in several human clinical trials across the country. *Photodynamic therapy* has recently shown promising results in the eradication of some cancer tumors through the use of laser beams. The procedure works by injecting the animal with an inactive cancer-killing drug known as a photosynthesizer. This drug travels throughout the body, incorporating itself into all the tissues, but concentrating especially in tumor tissue. When the laser beam is then directed at the tumor with this concentration of photosynthesizer drug, the drug undergoes a chemical change, releasing substances extremely toxic to cancer cells, thereby killing them. This dead tissue is then shed or sloughed off by the body in its own natural processes, requiring that the surgical site remain open for a time to allow for the seepage of fluids. Once the wound begins to exhibit signs of healing and the fluid production has stopped, the wound may be closed and skin grafts may be performed if the surgical site is an especially large area. To date, laser surgery for cancer tumors has produced far less negative complications than traditional radiation and chemotherapy. Common side effects seem to be swelling at the surgical site, loss of appetite, and lethargy. Unfortunately, it is not effective against all forms of cancer. Because the laser beam can only penetrate the body to about a depth of seven millimeters, it is a good surgical option for skin cancer, oral cancer, and soft tissue tumors but not for deep bone cancers or those involving many of the internal organs.

As of 1997, medical facilities that offered this type of radical new treatment to canines included the Animal Cancer Treatment Center of St. Clair Shores in Michigan, the University of Missouri/ Columbia, the University of California/Davis, and the Beckman Laser Institute at the University of California/Irvine. As the laser equipment becomes smaller and more affordable, more veterinary universities may begin offering laser treatment to their patients. Your regular veterinarian may be able to locate a teaching hospital in your area offering this service and possibly even a clinical trial for which your pet may qualify. It may be worth the time and effort to investigate this avenue of treatment.

In addition to amputation surgery, limb-sparing procedures, and the new and upcoming treatment options mentioned above, many dog owners are now also turning to alternative or holistic medicine in the care of their pets. Though this line of health care is by no means "cutting edge" and is in some cases quite ancient, many of these alternative treatments are finding strong supporters within the medical communities and even stronger advocates among the many patients (human and animal) who have benefited from them.

Holistic medicine is commonly defined as a system of medical care in which the health care provider considers the health of the whole animal, not just the symptoms of the disease. All aspects of the pet's life—physical, emotional, mental, and environmental—are closely examined and evaluated in order to determine the correct course of treatment for that individual. Alternative *medical treatments* (a term often used interchangeably with holistic medicine) are generally drug-free, non-surgical, Eastern practices. This is a vastly different system of care from traditional Western medicine, which relies almost entirely on surgery and some form of chemical or drug treatment. The one characteristic that almost all alternative medical treatments share is a belief that the body can heal or protect itself from disease if properly fed, aligned, stimulated, and supported. The only way to ensure that these needs are met is by providing proper nutrition, plenty of play and exercise, fresh air and exposure to appropriate amounts of sunlight, a conservative approach to vaccination and insect control, and a safe, loving, and stress-free environment in which to live. For those in need of more aggressive measures to help realign the body, mind, and spirit to proper equilibrium, alternative medical treatments such as chiropractics, acupuncture, massage, and homeopathy are available to pet owners in most parts of this country. In fact, a large number of amputee owners report that they use some form of alternative treatment in conjunction with traditional medicine for their pets.

As with any course of medical treatment, choosing to use a form of holistic medicine can be intimidating to those who know little about the various fields. An owner seeking to pursue alternative treatments for a sick pet must thoroughly investigate not only what might be the best course of action or treatment for the animal, but also who the individual is that will be performing such treatments. Preferably a practitioner will be a licensed veterinarian who has chosen to work in the field of alternative medicine. These individuals should possess certificates, degrees, licenses, or other measurable proof of their learning and knowledge within their particular field of study. Chiropractors and acupuncturists should be fully accredited, as should massage therapists, homeopaths, and nutritionists. If the individual to whom you are considering taking your pet for treatment cannot produce proof of his or her credentials that satisfy you, then find another provider. While those in the alternative medicine field are generally honest, caring, and dependable health care providers, one can encounter quacks and charlatans as in any other profession or trade. The Directory at the end of this book lists several sources for locating qualified professionals.

According to a Natural Pet Reader Survey (*Pet Supplies Marketing*, 1998) pet owners who use holistic treatments for their pets most commonly use the following types of alternative medicines:

61.0%	*Homeopathy*
55.2%	*Herbal Medicine*
54.3%	*Nutritional Therapy*
44.8%	*Flower Essences*
36.2%	*Touch Therapy (massage, etc)*
24.8%	*Acupuncture/Acupressure*
19.1%	*Chiropractic*
14.3%	*Other*

(Respondents often used more than one form of treatment.)

So what alternative treatments are best suited to canine amputees? Let's examine those most often mentioned by amputee owners as having been successful either in treating the overall health of the animal, providing comfort, or offering a reduction in pain or suffering.

The form of alternative medicine probably best known by most Americans is that of ***chiropractic medicine***. Once sneered at and even illegal to practice in many parts of the country, chiropractic medicine has proven itself as an effective and valuable form of treatment for both humans and animals. Today most human hospitals and health insurance companies offer or cover such treatments as routine medical care for their patients. Thousands of human and animal patients are treated every year by chiropractors for ailments such as arthritis, epilepsy, disk problems, nerve damage, behavior problems, and eating disorders.

Chiropractic therapy operates on the belief that disease conditions can exist in the body if there is an improper alignment of the body parts, thereby blocking the normal flow of energy, fluids, and nerve impulses. Such blockages can occur due to a traumatic injury (such as a car accident) or following years of debilitating disease (such as advancing arthritis). Chiropractic treatment seeks to rectify or eliminate these blockages by realigning the body parts properly.

Canine amputees who exhibit spinal subluxations or discomfort due to old injuries or due to the new manner in which they must now carry themselves as amputees, may find great relief in being periodically realigned by a qualified chiropractic vet. At the very least, it is a non-invasive, drug-free course of treatment that, when performed properly, does no harm to the animal even if no apparent change or benefit is readily perceived.

Acupuncture is a very ancient, Far Eastern practice with a basic premise similar to that of chiropractics. When the natural life force or energy (Chi) within the body is blocked or disrupted in some way, disease and sickness can occur. Acupuncture seeks to stimulate the flow of Chi and promote healing by inserting thin needles into very specific meridian points that affect various parts of the body. These thin needles are typically left in the body for ten to fifteen minutes. Some practitioners prefer to manipulate and spin the needles; others leave them alone, and still others may use heat or mild electrical impulses to stimulate the body's immune system. Acupuncture has been used to treat diseases such as cancer, arthritis, behavior problems, and diseases of the internal organs (liver, spleen, etc). Like chiropractics, when performed by a qualified professional, acupuncture is a very natural, non-harmful course of treatment. For many amputee owners, acupuncture has proven effective in controlling the spread of some cancers, extending some cancer survival rates and providing relief from painful conditions, alleviating muscle and nerve damage, treating appetite and eating problems, providing relief from arthritis conditions, and in general improving the overall health, spirit, and attitude of the animal.

Homeopathy is a very exacting branch of alternative medicine. First developed in the eighteenth century by Samuel Hahnemann and based on extremely ancient beliefs, its effectiveness has been rigorously tested, proven, and recorded. It is used alone and in conjunction with modern medical practices in almost all parts of the world with the exception, until recently, of the United States. (Homeopathy was used extensively in America in the 1800s, but with the arrival of the modern scientific era, homeopathic doctors were unfairly undermined, and the practice all but died out in this country.) Homeopathy operates under the belief that diseases or their symptoms can be cured by administering extremely dilute tinctures of a substance that actually produces the disease or symptoms. It is the belief of similars that "like can cure like." For example, a pet suffering from a variety of symptoms—perhaps weight loss, excessive shedding, lack of appetite, etc.—would be given a tincture of an herb, mineral, or animal-derived substance that was known to cause those exact same symptoms. Based on very specific guidelines, these tinctures are made safe by diluting them to such an extent that some hardly contain even a molecular trace of the original ingredient; they are believed to contain the healing energy of that original ingredient. This strict dilution process is known as the "Law of Minimal Dose."

A homeopathic veterinarian must be well versed not only in what effects certain substances can produce, but he or she must also know how to "read" that animal's mental, physical, and emotional states. Unlike modern medicine, which tends to break down all symptoms and treat each one separately (an aspirin for a headache, antibiotics for infection, steroids for an itchy rash), homeopathy addresses the health of the entire individual; it does not separate out each and every symptom to be treated by a different method, but strives to locate the one remedy that will best address all symptoms and the underlying cause of ill-health in that individual. Based on a thorough knowledge of homeopathic remedies and extensive experience in reading a pet's symptoms, the correct homeopathic treatments for a given condition generally work amazingly quickly and effectively. Almost any health problem occurring in pets can be addressed by homeopathy. This does not mean that the treatment will "cure" the disease or complication, but it may lessen its severity, improve the quality of life for the animal, or provide some form of relief. In this author's view, this field of medicine needs to be seriously revisited by American doctors (human and animal) and allowed to once again take its place alongside other forms of valuable medical treatments. The perfect form of health care would incorporate the best of both worlds—traditional and alternative treatments.

Touch therapy, which can include such treatments as massage and *Ttouch*, is finding a very beneficial place among the holistic practices offered to pet owners. Massage can help lower high blood pressure, stimulate blood flow, raise body temperature, encourage the release of endorphins (natural pain relievers and chemicals, which influence feelings of well-being), provide relief to sore or aching muscles, and encourage a more positive mental and emotional state of being, which in turn can assist in healing. All of these results are beneficial to the canine amputee. When seeking a massage therapist for treating your pet, be certain that that person has the credentials to perform the work he or she intends to do. Most certified animal massage therapists must first complete thorough training in the art of human massage before beginning their studies on animals. This important process enables the massage student to receive important feedback from the human patient regarding the effectiveness of the treatment. Because animals cannot vocalize their thoughts or opinions, the massage therapist must be very proficient and confident in his or her work on humans before applying it to a different species. This proficiency requires a complete knowledge of the muscular, skeletal, and nervous systems of the various species he or she may be called upon to treat.

Of course, many pets may find pleasure and relief in a simple massage provided by the owner. Just the act of stroking and caressing your pet from the tip of his nose to the end of his tail can be a wonderfully beneficial experience. It can also help detect changes or complications (such as lumps, bumps, or new tumors) in the animal's overall state of health. The owner should be sure to use firm motions with the correct amount of pressure for the pet's condition. Too light of a touch can tickle and irritate the animal, and applying too much pressure could further injure damaged tissue. Pets should not be forced to submit to massage. It must be a pleasurable experience for the animal and the owner. Little benefit will be derived if the owner spends the majority of the massage session attempting to wrestle the animal to the ground. Today, most literature on holistic pet care contains a chapter on massage techniques. The Directory at the end of this book can help you locate a source to get you started doing massage yourself or can help you locate a qualified massage specialist.

Ttouch, a system of pet massage developed by Linda Tellington Jones, targets the brain to produce specific brain-wave patterns, thereby influencing or changing behavior in the animal. This can be especially important in aggressive or dominant animals that suddenly find themselves in need of intensive health care, such as cancer treatments and wound or surgical site care. *Ttouch* can relax the animal, enabling the health care providers to perform their duties without unduly upsetting the animal or running the risk of injury to themselves or the pet. *Ttouch* practitioners, typically not veterinarians but general laypersons, must undergo a thorough course of study to be proficient in this form of therapeutic treatment. To a lesser degree, the average pet owner can also learn some of the general techniques to use immediately on his or her pet simply by studying the books and videos produced by Linda Tellington Jones. For information on locating a *Ttouch* practitioner or learning more about the technique yourself, see the Directory at the end of the book.

Pet owners today stand on the brink of a new age in the treatment of animal cancers and other medical complications. Traditional surgery, new techniques and drugs, and holistic medicine offer the pet owner a greater range of treatment than was ever before available. The courage that pet owners exhibit today in their relentless search for better health care for their animals will pave a way for even more incredible advances in medical treatment in the future. Perhaps one day diseases as serious as cancer may finally be controlled or altogether eradicated.

Chapter 13

Knowing When to Say Good-Bye

"Clarence"   *Photo Mary Kenney*

One of the saddest facts of being a pet owner is that we will outlive the majority of the animals with whom we share our lives. With the exception of parrots and tortoises, who may live to be one hundred years old, most pets have a very short lifespan of some ten to twenty years. A part of this hard reality is that we will ultimately have to decide when that pet's time on earth is done. Due to modern medicine, very few of our pets today simply drift peacefully away from us in their sleep. We attempt to use all the means at our disposal to prolong their lives and keep them with us. While we may do this because we love our pets deeply and cannot bear the thought of losing them, simply extending the *quantity* of life without taking into consideration the *quality* of that life is not necessarily a good thing. Science has given us the ability to extend life far beyond what may be morally or ethically responsible. It is our final act of caring for our pet to decide when that life must be extinguished.

Hospice care provides for the care of terminally ill patients in the comfort of their own homes prior to their deaths. Hospice services are typically provided by the owner or main caregiver with the cooperation of the attending veterinarian. The definition of a terminally ill patient is one that is believed to have less than six months left to live or one that has a progressive disease with quality of life issues to consider. The components of hospice care may include the control of pain, wound care, and aesthetic care (keeping the animal clean and providing means to deal with incontinence or vomiting). Toward this end, the owner must be certain that he or she is knowledgeable about all facets of the pet's condition, the level of care required, and whether he or she can confidently and accurately provide for those needs. If not, hospice care is not a suitable option for a pet owner.

Actions that the pet owner may be required to perform include the administration of medications (injections, topical treatments, and oral prescriptions), the control of bleeding, and/or the cleansing and odor control of wound sites, the ability to recognize and deal with situations such as seizures, fevers, and sleeplessness, and the willingness to attend to incontinence issues. In-home hospice care is becoming more widely accepted by the veterinary community, but there are still some vets who are reluctant to participate in this type of care due to their perceptions of legal risk to themselves and medical risk to the animal. Their fears are well founded. Hospice care is not an endeavor that should be approached lightly. It is a demanding type of care in which only the most dedicated and loving pet owners tend to participate. Pet owners should never attempt to provide hospice care on their own. If you feel that this type of care would be appropriate for you and your pet as he or she nears the end of life, schedule an appointment with your veterinarian in order to discuss the issue and determine the correct course of action. Keep in mind the inevitable, that your pet is dying. Your actions will in no way prompt a cure or remission. You are simply attempting to keep your pet happy and comfortable for as long as you possibly can.

A pet's quality of life is defined by his ability to care for himself and his enjoyment of his day-to-day activities. When examining the quality of an animal's life, the pet owner must make a serious assessment of several points.

- The ability of the pet to ambulate on his or her own and perform self grooming

- The ability to eat, enjoy the consumption of food, and benefit from the nutrition received

- The ability to perform normal bodily processes such as breathing and elimination

- The ability to enjoy everyday activities such as companionship and exercise

When these basic aspects of normal functioning become compromised by age or disease, the amount and type of decline must be evaluated in order to determine how the quality of that animal's life has been affected. A pet is known to have *clinical decline* if there is an increase in visits to the veterinarian, extended hospitalization, or a reduction in functional status. Animals that begin to exhibit changes in their ability to right themselves or get around, changes in appetite, changes in behavior or vocalization, incontinence, weight loss, anemia, and fluid retention or dehydration are showing signs of *functional decline.*

Other signs that the pet's quality of life has declined is a constant presence of pain, an inability to sleep, and no longer recognizing or caring to interact with the owner, in conjunction with clinical or functional declines. All these components point to the fact that the end is very near and the owner must make some hard decisions to put an end to unnecessary suffering.

Euthanasia is the compassionate ending of a pet's life when its pain has become unbearable or the quality of life has completely deteriorated. Euthanasia is most often accomplished by the administration of an anesthetic agent, which causes unconsciousness and a cessation of cardiac functions. This anesthetic is the same drug that is used to anesthetize animals for surgery, only given in larger doses. The anesthetic is commonly given as an intravenous injection, which works very quickly. But some veterinarians may not be opposed to giving the injection subcutaneously or even intramuscularly, thereby slowing the process down slightly for those pet owners who simply cannot bear to witness the sudden passing of their pet. Sub-Q and IM injections have the same effect as the intravenous injection; they just take a little longer to cause the cessation of cardiac function.

Pet owners may not be aware that some veterinarians will come to the home to perform euthanasia. Many owners simply cannot bear the thought of removing their pet from the comfort of his or her own surroundings and putting him or her to sleep in the cold, strange, sterile environment of the vet's office. They prefer to have the procedure done in their home, so that the animal may pass in peace and comfort, surrounded by the ones he or she loves. If your veterinarian does not perform these special house calls, do not be afraid to ask for a referral to one who does, or look through your local Yellow Pages until you find a vet who will perform this service.

Because euthanizing one's pet can be a very stressful and emotional experience, it is a good idea to have made some basic provisions for the pet's remains before the actual day that the procedure is performed. Most owners prefer to bury their pets at home. Families that have been in the same location for several generations may even have personal family pet cemeteries located on the property. Nowadays, pet owners should check the local zoning ordinances regarding the home burial of pets. Some communities allow it, while others do not. Home burials can provide a great deal of comfort to the owner, who cherishes knowing that the pet is still close by. Simple or elaborate burial sites and memorials can be erected on one's own property as well. Of course, a very important detail to consider is that home burial is the most inexpensive manner of interment.

There are several concerns that a pet owner may have when considering whether or not to bury the pet on the property. These include the fact that, at some time, the owner may sell the property and move away from the burial site or, if construction is planned for the property at any time down the road, the pet's final resting place may need to be disturbed. This can be an unacceptable possibility for many pet owners.

In these cases, pet owners may choose to have their beloved pet interred in a professionally run and maintained pet cemetery. These facilities are properly zoned and licensed just as a human cemetery is. As with human cemeteries, they offer a variety of plot locations and many different levels of grave care and upkeep. The costs for interment for a pet dog in a public facility begin at a few hundred dollars and range upward according to the services and options that the owner requests.

A pet cemetery is a very comforting place for most owners to visit, and it can help owners through the grieving process by enabling them to show respect for their pets through visiting and spending time there. Many owners create a special memorial day each year when they visit their pet and inspect the care of the grave and marker. To locate a pet cemetery in your area, see the Directory at the end of this book.

Other pet owners abhor the practice of burying their pet in the ground and prefer instead to have the animal's remains handled in a different manner. These owners choose *cremation* as an alternative to burial. According to Wallace Sife, PhD, in his book *The Loss of a Pet*, today approximately forty-five percent of deceased pets are cremated, and that number is rising.

Cremation for pets is similar to cremation for humans with one special exception. The pet owner may request that the pet's remains be processed in a private or public cremation. In a *private cremation*, the pet is cremated alone, and the ashes are returned to the owner in a simple urn. This service is generally performed through the local veterinarian, though it is acceptable for the owner to deliver the deceased pet directly to the crematorium. In a *public cremation*, the pet's remains are cremated "en masse" along with the remains of other pets. These ashes are not returned to the owners but are instead generally deposited in a suitable burial location on the crematorium's property. (Most facilities that operate a crematorium also operate a pet cemetery.) Public cremations may be requested by individuals who view the body simply as a shell for the soul and who have no emotional attachment to the physical remains. Public cremations may also be requested by those faced with financial restraints. Cremations are priced based on the weight of the animal, and because the ashes are not returned following a public cremation and therefore do not require special handling, the public cremation is less expensive than the private. Cremation fees for dogs start at around fifty dollars and can range upward into the several-hundred-dollar range depending on the animal's size and whether a public or private treatment is requested.

Personal pet cemeteries can be elaborate or simple to suit the owners' desires.
Photo Adele Guay

Many owners choose to keep their pet close by and opt for cremation, as did Marilyn Santoro when her beloved Mickey passed away at the age of thirteen. Mickey had undergone amputation at the ripe old age of eight to remove a malignant tumor on his front paw. He had five wonderful years of cancer-free living and finally succumbed to age-related complications. Mickey's ashes were interred in the screen house, which was his favorite place. The Santoro family takes comfort knowing that Mickey is always with them. For this reason, more and more pet owners choose cremation each year.

An important aspect of cremation is that it makes the pet's remains portable. In the event that the owner should move, he or she can simply and easily transport the reliquiae. Of course, the ashes themselves may always be buried should the owner so choose at a later date. Many owners like the fact the pet's ashes may be buried with the owner when their own time comes.

Some pet owners may choose alternatives to burial and cremation such as taxidermy, freeze drying, and mummification of the animal's remains. Though many pet owners may find these practices odd or unacceptable, these are procedures that have been practiced by cultures throughout the world for a variety of reasons. Only recently have such techniques become more widely available to owners as a means by which to preserve their treasured pet. In the end, personal sensibilities, practicality, and religious beliefs all play a part in which manner the individual chooses to handle his pet's remains.

After a pet's passing, many owners seek to provide some type of memorial for their beloved companion. Memorials can help relieve grief and provide a meaningful outlet for the pain that accompanies such loss. Gravestones and markers, whether for a home burial plot or a pet cemetery, provide a permanent mark of respect for the pet. Many owners plant a tree as a living memorial for the beloved pet. They can watch the tree grow, take care of it, and be reminded of the animal through all the seasons of the year. Some owners also erect a

plaque, dedicating the tree in the pet's memory. When Mitch Graham's Scottish Terrier, Randy, passed away, she not only laid him to rest beside her husband, who had passed away the year before, but she also planted a flowering shrub beside him as a living memorial.

If the dog was a show animal and competed in events such as hunting, herding, conformation, obedience, or agility you might try contacting your local kennel club about creating a memorial trophy in the dog's name. Most

Randy   *Photo Mitch Graham*   purebred dog clubs have newsletters or quarterly catalogs, and this is a fitting place to publish memorial notices. This provides a written record of your dog's passing, informs others who may have cared about the dog, and opens an avenue for friends who have been through the same ordeal to reach out and share their experiences with you. It often helps to know that you are not alone.

Donations in your pet's name can be made to local veterinary colleges and can even be targeted for specific causes (cancer research, amputation assistance for low-income pet owners, and pet loss support groups). Owners may also choose to make donations to local humane organizations or even establish college scholarships for veterinary students in their pets' memory. These are all wonderful ways in which to honor a loyal pet. Perhaps one of the simplest and most meaningful memorials can be created by starting a journal or remembrance book about your dog. Here the owner can record special memories about the dog, what his favorite type of treat was, with what toys he enjoyed playing, his best trick, or the funniest thing the dog ever did. Pictures, awards, and other mementos can be included in the book. In this way, a living record is set down honoring the life of that animal. It is a journal that the owner can refer back to time and again whenever he or she wishes to spend some quality time with his or her beloved companion. A pet owner has many resources available with which to honor and remember his or her pet; he or she is limited only by personal imagination and finances.

A very important aspect of a pet's passing is the involvement of the children. Caring parents who involve their children in some aspect of the pet's care prior to the end will be helping their children to prepare for the inevitable outcome. This will help the children understand just what is happening to their pet and make it easier for them to cope with their own loss. If the dog is truly considered a member of the family and is loved by the children, it is the parents' duty to involve them, at least to some extent, with the realities of the situation. Of course, children of different ages must be exposed to aspects of the pet's state of health and eventual death to a degree appropriate for their age. One thing to always remember is to be truthful with children. Do not lie. Never tell them that "Spot" ran away, went to live on Grandma's farm, was stolen, was given away, or is at the vet's. Discovering that they have been lied to about the death of their beloved pet is often far more damaging than simply being told the animal is very sick and will not live long.

Children should be allowed a chance to say good-bye to the pet in their own way. Most parents do not feel it necessary to have the children present during euthanasia, as this can be traumatic. However, they should be told the truth about the pet's condition, its suffering, and that the best alternative is to end the pain. Children today are much more mature than we were at their age. They understand and grasp concepts quicker. Due to their exposure to TV, the media, and video games, there are few who are not at least vaguely aware of death and the fact that eventually all things die. In agricultural societies—including our own at one time—children lived beside the daily realities of life and death. They watched the cattle and sheep and pigs be born, grow up, and ultimately become sustenance for the family. There was no great and terrible mystery about the cycle of life for farm children. Today's urban dwellers have become far removed from the agricultural lifestyle, to some degree out of touch with the realities of life and death. Some parents try to shield children from the natural processes, to keep them uninformed and childlike forever, but this can be a damaging road to follow. Children who do not learn at an early age how to accept loss and how to work through grief and disappointment seldom handle these stressful situations well as adults. They do not develop the emotional healing necessary that enables them to comprehend, assimilate, and process traumatic experiences like the loss of a loved one. It is an important lesson in any human's life and should not be denied. Limits to the degree to which the child is involved can certainly be established, but by completely denying that child the right to experience his or her own emotions and to learn how to deal with them, we do him or her an injustice.

The loss of a beloved pet, whether to old age or an incurable disease, is the hardest and most trying ordeal that any pet owner will experience. Every individual will handle the situation in his or her own unique way. Some pet owners, particularly those who are prepared for the inevitable and have made all their final preparations beforehand, accept the passing of their friend with quiet respect and sadness. Others, who are taken unaware by a sudden death or illness, may react with shock, guilt, blame, or anger. These are all normal reactions for humans to experience at the death of anyone they love—human or animal. *Grief* is the natural human response to a sudden, unexpected or overwhelming loss in one's life. Unfortunately, for a long time, some members of society have made pet owners feel that their grief is frivolous. As science delves deeper into the incredible bonds between humans and their animals, however, society is beginning to understand just how emotionally attached some people are to their pets. It is necessary for us to grieve for them when they leave us. There are several commonly accepted steps in the grieving process for humans.

- Shock / disbelief / denial
- Guilt or blame
- Depression
- Healing / acceptance

Not all stages of grief are experienced by all pet owners. Certain stages may be experienced in different degrees by different individuals. For example, the owner of a dog who has been ill with cancer may not experience the stages of shock, disbelief, guilt, or blame when that animal passes as he or she has been aware of the pet's condition for some time, knows what the inevitable outcome will be, and understands that there is nothing that can be done to save the dog's life. That owner may only experience the grief stages of depression and, in time, acceptance and healing. On the other hand, the owner who loses his dog suddenly, such as in a fatal car accident, may experience intense feelings of guilt, anger, and blame before moving on to the latter stages of grief. Likewise, may owners who lose their pets during surgery or while in the care of a veterinarian may experience intense feelings of denial and disbelief. They refuse to believe that their pet has died. They may request to see the body to determine that it truly is their pet; they may doubt that the veterinarian is telling the truth about the situation or claim that their pet actually ran away from the vet's office but did not die.

For those individuals suffering from the first two stages of grief, healing can take a very long time. There are many issues to work through before reaching a place where sadness and loss can be freely expressed and healing can begin. For these individuals and those who feel the need to discuss their situation with another caring soul who understands, there are several sources of support to which they may turn.

Pet Loss Support Groups and *hotlines* are available at many local and regional veterinary universities across the country. Most are staffed by veterinary students with varying hours of operation. They provide a welcome outlet for people to either get together in groups to discuss their shared experiences or allow for a more private conversation, one on one over the telephone. Some rescue shelters and humane organizations now also offer their own support groups. Pet owners in need of such a support system should check with their regular veterinarian about the location of a group in their local area.

Understanding friends and family members who are themselves pet owners can also provide a caring ear and a shoulder to cry on for those who have recently lost a beloved pet. The grieving owner should be judicious in his or her choice of friend in which to confide. People who do not own or love animals may, in some instances, make poor choices for sounding boards for our grief. They do not understand our intense feelings and can inadvertently hurt our feelings or cause greater pain to us through their lack of empathy.

For those individuals experiencing extreme, debilitating grief at the loss of a pet, professional counseling from a qualified doctor is recommended. Grief that affects a person so profoundly that he or she cannot function or carry out basic daily routines, has developed severe physical or psychological complications, or is contemplating thoughts of suicide, needs to be addressed immediately and by a licensed, experienced counselor. Such conditions should not be allowed to go untreated. The grieving pet owner must first be made to understand that there is no shame in seeking help to accept the loss of the pet. Humans have a profound ability to love beyond our own species, and it follows that, for some, feelings of loss and grief will be just as intense for a beloved pet as it would be for a human relative. It is all right to feel the way that we do about the death of our pets, but it is not all right to injure or harm ourselves over this loss. We are still alive and we have a responsibility to ourselves, our families, our friends, and to those animals that we may own in the future, to take care of ourselves and to be there for them when they need us.

It has been reported that some pets in the household may experience their own form of grief at the loss of one of their housemates. Behavior changes typically include loss of appetite, loneliness, nervousness or compulsive behavior (such as constantly searching for the missing housemate), vocalizing, changes in sleep patterns or locations, aggression toward other pack members (as in the case when the alpha dog in the household dies and the next in line is unsure of how to behave in his new position of power), and, in the case of older animals, death of the remaining one, though this is more typical with the loss of the human caretaker than with a housemate. Unfortunately, pets cannot be counseled and consoled in the same manner as humans. In these rare cases, the caring pet owner must be able to look beyond his or her own grief and provide love and support for the grieving pet. Many times the very act of caring for the remaining animal(s) in the house has a cathartic effect and assists the human in coming to terms with his or her own suffering and loss.

In experiencing and examining our grief over the loss of our pets, we are sometimes led down avenues of knowledge and enlightenment that we would otherwise not have traveled. Perhaps explorations of our religious options and the meaning of our pet's death will bring us not only comfort from better understanding ourselves and our pets, but also better understanding of our place in the divine scheme of things. In Wiccan beliefs (a northern European, nature religion) there is a tenant that everything in life happens for a reason, that there is a lesson to be learned from every experience, and that we must open our hearts, minds, and souls to the subtle or profound influences that these lessons may have on us. In accepting this belief, some would also acknowledge that the lesson to be learned from a pet's ordeal with cancer, amputation, or death may not have been a lesson intended for the owner's benefit. Quite possibly the lesson to be learned was part of the *pet's* life journey—the experience was the animal's alone. Though the situation may have a profound and lasting effect on humans, in many ways, the actual experience may have been a passage that the pet's spirit needed to make. The reasons for the lesson may never be revealed to the human caretakers, and that is all right. In the end, our pets will understand the meaning of the journeys they have taken. Perhaps when we meet them again after our own passing, they will impart to us all that they have learned.

Directory and Resources

"Rudy"   Photo Jenny Wendel

U.S. Universities with Colleges of Veterinary Medicine accredited by the AVMA

(Contact "School of Veterinary Medicine" at each individual college for information regarding oncology programs, orthopedic specialists, clinic trials, amputation surgeries, etc. Also call individual universities in your area to see if they offer pet loss support groups.)

Auburn University
Auburn University, Alabama 36849
(334) 844-3691
www.vetmed.auburn.edu

Tuskegee University
Tuskegee, Alabama 36088
(334) 727-8173
http://svmc107.tusk.edu/

University of California
Davis, California 95616-8734
(530) 752-1360
www.vetmed.ucdavis.edu

Western University of Health Services
309 E. Second St. College Plaza
Pamona, California 91766
(909) 469-5628
www.westernu.edu/cvm.html

Colorado State University
Fort Collins, Colorado 80523
(970) 491-7051
www.cvbs.colostate.edu

University of Florida
Gainesville, Florida 32610-0125
(352) 392-4700
www.vetmed.ufl.edu

University of Georgia
Athens, Georgia 30602
(706) 542-3461
www.vet.uga.edu

University of Illinois
2001 S. Lincoln
Urbana, Illinois 61801
(217) 333-2760
www.cvm.uiuc.edu

Purdue University
1240 Lynn Hall
West Lafayette, Indiana 47907-1240
(765) 494-7607
www.purdue.edu

Iowa State University
Ames, Iowa 50011
(515) 294-1242
www.vetmed.iastate.edu

Kansas State University
Manhattan, Kansas 66506
(785) 532-6011
www.vet.ksu.edu

Louisiana State University
Baton Rouge, Louisiana 70803
(225) 346-3100
www.vetmed.lsu.edu

Virginia Tech & University of Maryland
Blacksburg, Maryland 24061-0442
(540) 231-4621
www.vetmed.vt.edu

Tufts University
200 Westboro Rd.
N. Grafton, Massachusetts 01536
(508) 839-5302
www.tufts.edu/vet

Michigan State University
East Lansing, Michigan 48824-1314
(517) 355-6509
www.cvm.msu.edu

University of Minnesota
St. Paul, Minnesota 55108
(612) 624-9227
www.cvm.umn.edu

Mississippi State University
Mississippi State, Mississippi 39762
(662) 325-3432
www.cvm.msstate.edu

University of Missouri
Columbia, Missouri 65211
(573) 882-3877
www.cvm.missouri.edu

Cornell University
Ithaca, New York 14853-6401
(607) 253-3700
www.vet.cornell.edu

North Carolina State University
4700 Hillsboro St.
Raleigh, North Carolina 27606
(919) 513-6200
www2.ncsu.edu/ncsu/cvm/cvmhome.html

Ohio State University
Columbus, Ohio 43210
(614) 292-1171
www.vet.ohio-state.edu

Oklahoma State University
Stillwater, Oklahoma 74078
(405) 744-6648
www.cvm.okstate.edu

University of Pennsylvania
3800 Spruce St.
Philadelphia, Pennsylvania 19104-6044
(215) 898-5434

University of Tennessee
Knoxville, Tennessee 37901
(865) 974-7262
www.vet.utk.edu

Texas A & M University
College Station, Texas 77843-4461
(409) 845-5051
www.cvm.tamu.edu

Washington State University
Pullman, Washington 99164-7010
(509) 335-9515
www.vetmed.wsu.edu

University of Wisconsin-Madison
Madison, Wisconsin 53706
(608) 263-6716
www.vetmed.wisc.edu

Oregon State University
Corvallis, Oregon 97331-4801
(541) 737-2141
www.vet.orst.edu

To Locate A Veterinarian Practicing Alternative Medicine

Homeopathy:

Academy for Veterinary Homeopathy
751 NE 168th St.
N. Miami, FL 33162-2427
(305) 652-5372

International Association for Veterinary Homeopathy
334 Knollwood Lane
Woodstock, GA 30188
(770) 516-7622

Holistic/Herbal:

American Holistic Veterinary Medical Association (AHVMA)
2218 Old Emmorton Rd.
Bel Air, MD 21014
(410) 569-0795
www.altvetmed.com

Georgia Holistic Veterinary Medical Association
334 Knollwood Lane
Woodstock, GA 30188
(770) 516-5954

Rocky Mountain Holistic Veterinary Medical Association
311 S. Pennsylvania St.
Denver, CO 80209
(303) 733-2728

Mid-Western Holistic Veterinary Medical Association
(608) 255-1239

Greater Washington DC Area Holistic Veterinary Assoc.
6136 Brandon Ave.
Springfield, VA 22150
(703) 503-8690

Acupuncture:
International Veterinary Acupuncture Society
PO Box 271395
Fort Collins, CO 80527
(970) 266-0666

Center for Veterinary Acupuncture
1405 West Silver Spring Dr.
Glendale, WI 53209
(800) 680-2282

American Academy of Veterinary Acupuncture
PO Box 419
Hygiene, CO 80533-0419
(303) 772-6726

Chiropractic:
American Veterinary Chiropractic Association (AVCA)
623 Main St.
Hillsdale, IL 61257
(309) 658-2920
AmVetChiro@aol.com

Touch Therapy:
Tellington Touch Therapy/Ttouch and T.TE.A.M.
PO Box 3793
Santa Fe, NM 87501
(800) 854-8326
www.tteam-ttouch.com

Other:
Veterinary Institute for Therapeutic Alternatives
15 Sunset Terrace
Sherman, CT 06784
(860) 354-2287
Teaches veterinarians about alternative veterinary medicine

Animal Natural Health Center
1283 Lincoln St.
Eugene, OR 97401
(541) 342-7665
office@drpitcairn.com

Support Groups/Newsletters For Disabled Pets

Dogs with Disabilities (newsletter)
1406 East Small Lane
Mt. Prospect, IL 60056
(847) 296-8277
Fax (847) 296-8210
dwd@bytemeusa.com

Canine Sports Medicine Update (newsletter)
PO Box 351
Newmarket, NH 03857

Your Dog Newsletter by Tufts University
PO Box 420272
Palm Coast, FL 32142
(800) 829-5116

Support Websites:

AltaVista Search Engine: "Cassie's Three-legged Dog Club" or
http://lark.cc.ukans.edu~kurdavis/doghome.html

Yahoo! Search Engine: Yahoo Groups "Special Needs Pets Support"
Special-Needs-Pets-Support@yahoogroups.com

www.ivillage.com/pets
www.rainbowark.com
www.forpetloversonly.com

Pet Hospice Organization

Nikki Hospice Foundation for Pets
Rosemoor House
400 New Bedford Dr.
Vallejo, CA 94591
(707) 557-8595/Fax (707) 557-5555
www.csum.edu\pethospice

National Therapy Dog Organizations

These organizations train and certify dogs and their owners to do therapy work. For a complete listing of local Therapy Dog Associations: www.golden-retriever.com/therapy

Therapy Dogs Inc.
PO Box 5868
Cheyenne, WY 82003
(307) 432-0272
www.therapydogs.com

Delta Society
289 Perimeter Rd. East
Renton, WA 98055-1329
(425) 226-7357
www.deltasociety.com

Dog Clubs and Organizations That Welcome Amputees

United Kennel Club Inc.
100 East Kilgore Rd.
Portage, MI 49002-5584
(616) 343-9020

Amputees are allowed to compete in UKC licensed agility, obedience, and hunting tests. No conformation class.

International Federation of Canines
PO Box 250307
Montgomery, AL 36125-0307
(334) 284-4838
FICREGSTRY@aol.com
www.ficregistry.org

Amputees allowed to compete in obedience, dog sport, good citizen, temperament tests, tracking, and agility

Animal Research & Funding Organizations

AKC Canine Health Foundation
251 W. Garfield Rd., Suite 160
Aurora, Ohio 44202-8856
(330) 995-0807
(888) 682-9696
www.akcchf.org
Various studies and trials relating to many different diseases, including cancer

Morris Animal Foundation
45 Inverness Drive East
Englewood, CO 80112-5480
(800) 243-2345
(303) 790-4066 fax (303) 790-2345
A funding source for animal health studies conducted at veterinary institutions throughout the world.

Ongoing programs of interest to amputee/cancer patient owners include:

- *Cancer Diets*
- *Cancer Genetics*
- *Cancer Registry*
- *Osteosarcoma (several studies)*
- *Melanoma (several studies)*
- *Tumor Therapy*
- *Medical Therapy*

Veterinary Cancer Society
PO Box 1763
Spring Valley, CA 91979-1763
(619) 460-2002 fax(619) 741-1117

To Make Donations to VCS:
VCS Fund of the Amer. Veterinary Medical Foundation
1931 N. Meacham Rd.
Schaumburg, IL 60173

The VetCancer Registry
PO Box 352
168 West Main St.
New Market, MD 21774
Email and FAX numbers for veterinary submission of cytology, necropsy or biopsy reports only:

info@vetcancerregistry.com
301-695-9179

Human Research Organizations

National Cancer Institute
Office of Cancer Communications
31 Center Drive, MSC 2580
Bethesda, MD 20892-2580
(800) 422 6237
(301) 435-3848
www.cancer.gov

National Amputation Foundation
38-40 Church St.
Malverne, NY 11565
(516) 887-3600
Fax (516) 887-3667
www.nationalamputation.org
National non-profit organization serving the needs of human amputees. They produce many pamphlets and brochures that the owner of the canine amputee may find useful.

Helpful Supply Sources For Canine Amputees

CanineAmputeeSupply.com

Internet site devoted to canine amputees. Useful supplies and unique gifts and books for amputees and their owners

Cart/Harness/Sling Manufacturers

K-9 Cart Co.
656 SE Bayshore Dr. Suite 2
Oak Harbor, WA 98277-5739
(360) 675-1808
(800) 578-6960
www.k9carts.com

Doggon Wheels
PO Box 1503
Livingston, MT 59047
(888) 736-4466
www.doggon.com

Dewey's Wheelchairs for Dogs
PO Box 9370
Bend, OR 97708
(877) 312-2122
www.wheelchairsfordogs.com

Northland Newfoundland Club
c/o Helen Mancuso
227 Roaser Rd.
Sand Lake, NY 12153
(518) 674-3393

Slings of durable nylon pack cloth, padded with berber fleece. Call for pricing and order form.

Stairs and Ramps

PetSTEP Inc. (dog steps)
PO Box 6488
San Mateo, CA 94403
(877) PET-STEP
(650) 574-4760
www.petstep.com

C & D Pet Products Inc.(dog steps)
405 E D St.
Petaluma, CA 94952-3177
(888) 554-7387
(707) 763-1654
www.cdpets.com

Smith-Kruger Inc. (pet bed ramps)
4488 Candelberry Ave.
Seal Beach, CA 90740-3025
(877) 327-5438
(562) 460-6134
www.bedderbacks.com

I.Q. Industries Inc. (pet car ramps)
11111 Biscayne Blvd. Suite 315
Miami, FL 33181-3404
(877) 364-5438
(866) 364-7267
www.dogramp.com

Helpful Web Pages

The author reminds readers that these sites may or may not still be in existence at the time of publication. Many of the sites are human-related, but useful general information can still be acquired by dog owners.

American Kennel Club/Canine Health Foundation
  www.akc.org/chf
American Veterinary Medical Association
  www.avma.org
Association of American Veterinary Medical Colleges
  www.aavmc.org
Morris Animal Foundation
  www.morrisanimalfoundation.org
National Institute of Health
  www.nih.gov
National Cancer Institute/CancerNet
  www.cancernet.nci.nih.gov
Purina Pet Foods
  www.purina.com
Veterinary Cancer Society
  www.vetcancersociety.org
University of Pennsylvania's "Oncolink"
  www.upenn.edu
North Carolina Animal Cancer Treatment Program
  www.cvm.ncsu.edu
Human Cancer Resource Sites:
  www.cancerlinksusa.com
  www.cancerdirectory.com
  www.oncoweb.8m.com
  www.cancerbacup.org.uk/
  www.cancerindex.org/clinks1.html
  http://seidata.com/~marriage/rcancer.html
National Cancer Institute/CancerNet
  www.cancernet.nci.nih.gov

Pet Insurance Companies

America

Veterinary Pet Insurance Co.
PO Box 68052
Anaheim, CA 92817-9905
Fax (714) 985-0525
(800) 872-7387
www.petinsurance.com

Pet Assure Holdings Inc.
10 S. Morris St.
Dover, NJ 07801
(888) 789-PETS
Fax (973) 537-9868
www.pctassurc.com

Premier Pet Insurance
9541 Harding Blvd.
Wauwatosa, WI 53226
(877) 774-2273
www.ppins.com

Healthy Pets Insurance
www.healthy-pets.com

Canada

Pet Plan Insurance
777 Portage Ave.
Winnipeg, MB R3G ON3
(800) 268-1169
(204) 943-0331
www.petplan.com

Pet Loss

Support

Association for Pet Loss & Bereavement
PO Box 106
Brooklyn, NY 11230
(718) 382-0690
www.aplb.org
Provides counseling, meetings, and lists of support groups by state

Pet Loss Support Group
School of Veterinary Medicine
2015 Linden Dr.
Madison, WI 53706
(608) 836-PAWS

AMVA On-Line Support Information
www.avma.org/pet loss

Super Dog's Pet Loss Reference Site
www.superdog.com/petloss.htm

Iams Pet Loss Support Resource Center
(888) 332-7738

Others:

www.pet-loss.net
www.petloss.com
Also contact schools of veterinary medicine at local universities. Most maintain a pet loss support hotline staffed by students and medical staff.

Memorials Websites

www.In-Memory-Of-Pets.com
www.dogheaven.com
www.petmemories.com
www.mycemetery.com
www.rainbowbridge.com

To Locate a Pet Cemetery or Crematorium

International Association of Pet Cemeteries
2845 Oakcrest Place
Land O' Lakes, FL 34639
www.lapc.com

Suppliers of pet urns, caskets, and markers

My Pet Casket Company
(800) 714-9232
(704) 948-8617
www.mypetcasket.com

Blue Ribbons
1442 Peters Blvd.
Bay Shore, NY 11706-3946
(800) 552-2583
(516) 968-9164
www.blueribbonspetcare.com

www.discounturns.com
(888) 876-7888

T & S Pet Memorials
PO Box 5173
Ocean Isle Beach, NC 28469
(910) 575-2943
www.tsmemorials.com

My Cherished Pet
c/o Design Cast Studios
1245 Center St.
Henderson, KY 42420
(888) 830-6412
www.mycherishedpet.com

Reflections Pet Urns
6218 33rd. St. North
St. Petersburg, FL 33702
(800) 546-4164
(727) 528-PETS
www.peturns.com

Hoegh Pet Casket Co.
PO Box 311
Gladstone, MI 49837
(906) 428-2151
www.abka.com/hoegh

Highly Recommended Holistic/All-Natural Dog Food Manufacturers

(Dry and canned food, supplements, treats, etc.)

PetGuard Foods
165 Industrial Loop, South
Orange Park, FL 32073
(800) 874-3221
(800) 331-7527 (in Florida)
www.petguard.com

Solid Gold Holistic Animal Nutrition Center
1483 N. Cuyamaca St.
El Cajon, CA 92020-1508
(619) 258-7356
www.solidgoldhealth.com

Halo, Purely for Pets
3438 E. Lake Rd. Suite 14, PMB 612
Palm Harbor, FL 34685-2413
(800) 426-4256
www.halopets.com

Innova Dog Food
by Natura Pet Products
1101 S. Winchester Blvd. Suite J225
San Jose, CA 95128-3919
(800) 532-7261
(408) 261-0770
www.naturapet.com

Wysong Corp.
1880 N. Eastman Rd.
Midland, MI 48642-8901
(517) 631-0009
www.wysong.com

Neura Wellness by Old Mother Hubbard
80 Rogers St. PO Box 1719
Lowell, MA 01853-1719
(800) 225-0904
www.oldmotherhubbard.com

Bibliography

Anderson, N. & H. Peiper. *Are You Poisoning Your Pets?* East Canaan, Connecticut: Safe Goods, 1995.

Bognar, D. *Cancer: Increasing Your Odds for Survival.* Alameda, Calif.: Hunter House, 1998.

Carlson, D. & J. Giffin. *Dog Owner's Home Veterinary Handbook.* New York: Howell Book, 1980.

Coren, S. *The Intelligence of Dogs.* New York: Bantam Press, 1994.

Department of Veteran Affairs. *Things to Know About Amputation and Artificial Limbs.* New York: National Amputation Foundation, 1994.

Dollinger, M., E. Rosenbaum, G. Cable. *Everyone's Guide to Cancer Therapy.* Ontario, Canada: Somerville House Books, 1997.

Fishman, S. *Psychological Practices with the Physically Disabled (Amputation).* Reprinted. New York: National Amputation Foundation, 1961.

Melzack, R. *Phantom Limbs.* New York: National Amputation Foundation reprint from *Scientific American,* April, 1992.

Moussaieff Masson, J. & S. McCarthy. *When Elephants Weep: The Emotional Lives of Animals.* New York: Delacorte Press, 1995.

Moussaieff Masson, J. *Dogs Never Lie About Love.* New York: Crown Publishing, 1997.

Ogilvie, G. & A. Moore. *Managing the Veterinary Cancer Patient*. Trenton, New Jersey: Veterinary Learning Systems, 1995.

Pitcairn, R. & S. Pitcairn. *Dr. Pitcairn's Complete Guide to Natural Health for Dogs & Cats*. Emmaus, Pennsylvania: Rodale Press, 1995.

Sife, W. *The Loss of a Pet*. New York: Howell Book, 1993.

Stein, D. *Natural Healing for Dogs & Cats*. Freedom, California: The Crossing Press, 1993.

Thurston, M.E. *The Lost History of the Canine Race*. Kansas City, Missouri: Andrews and McMeel, 1996.

Volhard, W. & K. Brown. *The Holistic Guide for a Healthy Dog*. New York: Howell Book, 1995.

Walkey, B. *The Bullmastiff Fancier's Manual*. British Columbia, Canada: Coast Arts Publishing, 1992.

Walkowicz, C. & B. Wilcox. *Successful Dog Breeding: The Complete Handbook of Canine Midwifery*. New York: Howell Book, 1994.

Index

YOU
can make a
Difference
in the lives of abandoned and abused animals in the central Illinois area.

Foster Pet OutReach

Helping Animals In Need

Peg

If we sat around a table and developed adoptability standards, a
middle-aged Pit Bull with only 3 legs probably wouldn't make the cut.
But working in the kennels, touching and being touched by each dog,
gives us a different perspective.

We saw in Peg a gallant old gal, whose ability to offer love and to
long for it was in no way diminished by her breed or the loss of a leg.
Roxie Brophy saw what we saw and told us her friends Dave and
Millie Davis had lost a beloved dog and might have room in their
hearts for our Peg.

It's been a few years now since Peg found the wonderful home she
deserved. That's a long time in a dog's short life, and she has made the
most of every moment. May the spirit that kept her tail up and
wagging through the loneliness and the pain surround her in
joy forever.

DAWG

Dog Adoption & Welfare Group

*Serving the Dogs of the
Santa Barbara County Shelter*

Turbo wastes no time getting outside
after having his prosthetic paw readjusted.
He pulls his owner, Willie Hamm, along.
In back watching is *Jesse Rowley,*
a practitioner's assistant at NovaCare
Orthotics & Prosthetics in Fredericksburg,
where the paw was constructed.

Stafford Star, October 1997

The Region

Buford, a 14-week-old Labrador-springer spaniel, tries out his new artificial leg under the watchful eye of owner Pam Scott, who found him at the Josephine County Animal Shelter in Grants Pass, Ore., already missing the limb.